Detroit Ghosts

Mimi Staver

Schiffer Publishing Ltd®

4880 Lower Valley Road, Atglen, Pennsylvania 19310

Cover photo:American City Skyline and Waterfront©Ivan Cholakov. Image from BigStockPhoto.com

Other Schiffer Books by the author:
Ann Arbor Area Ghosts, 978-0-7643-2850-3, $14.95

Other Schiffer Books on Related Subjects:
Ghosts of Anchor Bay, 0-7643-2302-4, $9.95

Schiffer Books are available at special discounts for bulk purchases for sales promotions or premiums. Special editions, including personalized covers, corporate imprints, and excerpts can be created in large quantities for special needs. For more information contact the publisher:

Schiffer Publishing Ltd.
4880 Lower Valley Road
Atglen, PA 19310
Phone: (610) 593-1777; Fax: (610) 593-2002
E-mail: Info@schifferbooks.com

For the largest selection of fine reference books on this and related subjects, please visit our web site at **www.schifferbooks.com.** We are always looking for people to write books on new and related subjects. If you have an idea for a book please contact us at the above address.

This book may be purchased from the publisher.Include $5.00 for shipping. Please try your bookstore first. You may write for a free catalog.

In Europe, Schiffer books are distributed by:

Bushwood Books
6 Marksbury Ave.
Kew Gardens
Surrey TW9 4JF England
Phone: 44 (0) 20 8392-8585; Fax: 44 (0) 20 8392-9876
E-mail: info@bushwoodbooks.co.uk
Website: www.bushwoodbooks.co.uk
Free postage in the U.K., Europe; air mail at cost.

Type set in Bard/NewsGoth BT

ISBN: 978-0-7643-3179-4
Printed in United States of America

Dedication

This book is dedicated to my daughter, Samantha,
for her energy and inspiration.

I shall be telling this with a sigh
Somewhere ages and ages hence:
Two roads diverged in a wood, and
I—I took the one less traveled by,
And that has made all the difference.

-- Robert Frost, "The Road Not Taken," 1916

Acknowledgments

I would like to extend my gratitude to the Magnificent Seven, and to the Divine, without whom this book would not be possible. And to my dearest friend Anita, who is a constant source of strength. My appreciation also goes out to my siblings: Danielle, Frank, and Dennis, as well as their spouses.

Contents

Introduction

Since I was a young child, the subject of ghosts has always fascinated me. I was born and raised in Detroit, along with my three siblings, and we shared our home with a resident ghost. This prompted my interest in the paranormal, beginning around age nine. Often times, a combination of wicked, winter storms and ancient electrical wiring in our 1900s home caused blackouts, which resulted in four bored kids with nothing to do but let our imagination get the best of us. Little did we know that made-up stories about a weird neighbor, whom we referred to as, "The Lady of the Cornfield," or the troublesome trio of ghosts in our grandparents' home on Hereford Street, which we affectionately referred to as "The Carson Brothers," would lay the groundwork that spawned my interest in studying the real ghosts of Detroit.

I was lucky enough to be exposed to a wide range of history and culture. My father spent thirty-two years working in a Detroit museum and I watched him regale stories and bits of history to eager visitors. He enjoyed taking me and my siblings to the Detroit Historical Museum, Dossin Great Lakes Museum, local libraries, old monasteries, Tiger Stadium, and other Detroit landmarks. Childhood memories of the Motor City include the civil unrest during the Detroit Riots, celebrating the World Series, quick trips to Canada via the tunnel, freighters on Lake St. Clair, drag races down Woodward Avenue (the first concrete highway in America), and other ups and downs that made Detroit the tough, surviving city that keeps its spirit alive, no matter the odds.

Perhaps the culmination of my appreciation for culture and interest in things that go bump in the night served a purpose—to write about the city with an approach from a road not taken—the dark side. I amassed a great deal of eyewitness reports, helped lead investigations into a few spooky places, and gathered twisted tales from the past. My sister, Danielle, shared her enthusiasm and insight of the city's cultural gems and her historical knowledge of Henry Ford's Greenfield Village, and other local attractions. My brother Dennis has an amazing ability to retain trivia about Detroit cemeteries and little-known facts about prominent figures of Detroit's past, and he helped me dig up the dirt on both. My brother Frank offered two leads to hauntings on the east side, of which you will read about in *Chapters Five* and *Ten*, and loaned me an antique reference book that proved to be of significant importance in researching the old buildings of Detroit. The four of us have remained close since we left our old childhood home, and this book is a tribute to them.

I highly suggest you pour yourself a nice cup of your favorite beverage and curl up in your favorite chair. Imagine a city once inhabited by millionaires and automotive pioneers...some who still refuse to leave. Picture a town that was nearly wiped out by a Cholera epidemic in the 1800s. Imagine a city with a large fort that was taken over from the British by a rebellious Chief Pontiac in the 1700s, during the French and Indian War. Visit old pubs and factories where tough proprietors still oversee day-to-day business transactions. Enjoy *Detroit Ghosts*, and gain further insight about what happens on the dark side when the lights go out in the Motor City. As always, I wish you and yours happy hauntings. Welcome to Detroit.

1

Corktown

"A house is never still in darkness to those who listen intently; there is a whispering in distant chambers, an unearthly hand presses the snib of a window, the latch rises. Ghosts were created when the first human awoke in the night."

-- J. M. Barrie

Detroit's oldest settled neighborhood, near the downtown area, is an Irish community referred to as Corktown. The area evolved due to the rush of Irish immigrants seeking a new life during Ireland's potato famine in the 1840s. The opening of the Erie Canal brought Irish immigrants into New York, Chicago, Ohio, and Detroit. Carpenters, dockworkers, and other hard workers were needed and the immigrants were more than happy to become permanent citizens. And with plenty of housing to be built to shelter the large Irish families, lumber and woodworking jobs were available. A handful of the long, simple worker's row houses, usually built in close proximity to each other, can still be seen in the neighborhood. Some of the remaining few have been preserved and remodeled to reflect the character of the first immigrants from Cork County, Ireland, where the Corktown neighborhood earned its name. The homes were designed in a pattern dating back three hundred years, and each home was sectioned out in narrow twenty-five-foot lots.

But not all of the homes in Corktown were row houses. In fact, some of the well-built Victorian homes on the outskirts of Corktown still exist today. I had the pleasure of visiting the owner of one of those homes. The beautiful residence was, at one time, a sportsman's club, where its members truly enjoyed social gatherings. The social gatherings were so enjoyable that the members return on a regular basis, *in spirit form*. My other visit to Corktown, in conjunction with an investigation by the Michigan Investigations and Research of the Paranormal team, involved some spooky happenings at a pub called Nancy Whiskey. Enjoy these stories from the oldest neighborhood in the city.

The Sportsman's Club

The cigar smoke, the tinkling of glasses, the shuffling of footsteps, and the sound of hearty conversation is only part of what C. J. experiences around the fireplace on cold winter nights in her Victorian home near 12th Street in Detroit. Lucky for C. J., there is no time spent cleaning up, no spilled scotch on the antique furniture, and no cigar ashes to dump out after the party guests go home. The visitors in the home leave no trace that they were ever there…*because they weren't*.

Built in 1890, the home was occupied by at least two families at different intervals before it became a sportsman's club in 1930. Remnants of a storage area on the rear of the property can still be seen—a brick structure with bays that may have once housed cars or boats. Decades-old water and electric hookups are still visible before the sportsman's club left the building in 1967.

Perhaps somehow the whirlwind of activity is connected to the buying and selling of the home. The lengthy time as a sportsman's club ended in a sea of anarchy, when an incident at an after hours drinking club at nearby 12th Street set off a chain of events that would be forever known as the 1967 Detroit Riots. By the end of the five-day riot, forty-three people were dead, 1,189 were injured, and over 7,000 arrests were made. Looting and fires swept across the city. Homes and buildings in the area were raided, abandoned, or used as shelters. And the gentlemen of the sportsman's club took flight, leaving the historical building with its fireplace, polished wood staircase, and ornate exterior.

Three years later, a gentleman named Charlie bought the home, moved in, and remained there for the next thirty years, until C. J. and her husband bought it. When C. J. tells me about the first time the real estate agent showed the home to her and her husband, I wonder about the odd events that seem connected somehow with whirlwind activity. C .J. states that the realtor had taken her on a tour of the home and, as she crossed over the threshold and entered the foyer, she was instantly hit by a panic attack. She thought that maybe she was just nervous about the possible impending purchase, though she states that she never had a panic attack before. "I didn't want to buy the house," C. J. tells me. "My husband wanted to buy it. He was instantly connected to it. But it was in pretty bad shape and was really in need of some major cleaning. The wood floors needed so much work." In regards to ghosts, C. J. states that she had not heard of anything out of the ordinary there, and that there was a rumor that a little girl had died in the house…nothing really outstanding as far as history and ghosts. C. J. was more concerned about the physical condition of the home. She adds, "But life is about taking risks, and I just decided to go for it."

It was a special day for the couple on the day they signed the documents purchasing the home from Charlie, who was suffering the effects of a lengthy illness. That day, C. J. and her husband became the official owners of the Victorian home. A few hours later, it would prove to be a strange day indeed. Upstairs, in the master bedroom of the home, Charlie laid down in the bed facing the upstairs window—and never woke up. But that was just one strange event. Outside, trouble was brewing.

The day started out to be a sunny July morning, just a couple weeks shy of the 30th anniversary of the 1967 riots that made the gentlemen at the former sportsman's club leave town. Moods were high, as the long-awaited Fourth of July weekend dawned and C. J. and her husband were congratulating themselves as new homeowners. The skies over Michigan became overcast by noon. At 2 o'clock in the afternoon the wind picked up and was soon followed by a torrential downpour. By 3:30, the first of sixteen tornadoes began tearing through the state. When it was over, more than seven people had been killed and damages totaled more than $135 million. Dear Charlie lay dead upstairs and the highest amount of tornadoes in a single day in Michigan's history had just occurred. How's that for a first day as a homeowner?

But the house survived and it wasn't long before they moved in and began the tough road ahead of them—getting the house in shape. *And the spirits seemed to come out of the woodwork.*

"Right away," C. J. says, "it was one thing after another... nonstop. And always, even now, there is the constant feeling of being watched."

One of the first occurrences happened in the living room, where C. J. states that she still recalls the incident in detail... the day her two-year-old son began showing signs of fear without any real explanation. "He would duck down and point upwards, saying 'there...there' and would cry." When

A rear view of the former sportsman's club on Hancock, in Detroit's Corktown district.

he began to form sentences at about age three, C. J.'s son would chatter about a mommy who could fly. C. J. asked her son how he knew this and the boy would respond that the 'mommy' talks to him. The spirit told him that at one time, a long time ago, she hurt herself and had the capability to move to different places in the house…basically the woman had the ability [at least through a child's understanding] to fly. She could appear anywhere at anytime.

C. J. accompanied a friend on a trip to Vermont where they decided to visit a medium, who C. J. did not know and who knew nothing about the situation. The medium told C. J. that she picked up the spirit of a woman in the home—a woman who died in childbirth. It's interesting to note that perhaps the spirit of the woman hangs out because she can relate to C. J. and her son in special way—when C. J. was pregnant with her son, she decided to forgo giving birth in a hospital and had the baby at home. "The spirit is there to tie up some loose ends," the medium told C. J. That bit of news was enlightening, but was of little help to C. J., who was constantly consoling her fearful toddler besieged by a 'flying mommy.'

It was then that the medium told her to confront the spirit and say, "You can stay and we can live in harmony, or you're going to have to leave. Because I am staying. I will not have my family upset by you." For a long time after that, it got quiet, but C. J. says, "The overt activity discontinued, but not the subtleties."

In the upstairs bedroom, where Charlie took his last breath, was where most of the odd activity occurred. One evening, half dozing on the bed, which was actually a futon with a low frame close to the floor, C. J. felt a tugging motion at the side of the bed. The tugging motion evolved into what appeared to her as a pair of child's hands that began pushing the futon mattress from one side, where C. J. was sleeping, to the opposite side, where C. J.'s husband was sound asleep. In a state of shock, she suddenly found herself nearly thrown to the other side of the bed where she landed on top of her surprised husband. Not long afterwards, more child spirit activity occurred in the same room.

She tells me about an incident when a peaceful day was interrupted by a noisy child playing ball in the house:

> "I was on the main floor of the house and all was quiet. I began to hear a loud, constant bumping sound coming from upstairs. It had a rhythm to it. Bumpity-bump, bumpity-bump. It kept repeating itself over and over."

Knowing full well that none of the family members were upstairs, C. J.'s curiosity got the best of her and she crept

13

upstairs to find the reason for the rhythmic bumping noise. She describes the scene that unfolded in front of her:

> "I saw a white ball, moving up and down, bouncing by itself by unseen hands. And I saw what I can only explain as the shadowy appearance of the after effects caused by the movement of the ball, whenever it bounced up and down. There was no one there. I was so shocked to see this ball just bouncing by itself. I knew there was no white ball in the house. It completely caught me off guard."

As C. J. remain transfixed on the image, it began to fade. "At this point, I really wanted to interact with the ghost to find out who it is. I tried to remain calm, but the bouncing ball was so shocking. And when I reacted, that's when it faded away," she says.

I explained to C. J. that it's unfortunate the ball disappeared, because it would have been intriguing to analyze the toy. What this homeowner experienced is a paranormal incident involving an **apport**—the appearance of a solid object transferred by and through an unknown source. It would have been amazing to have that tangible object to analyze. Often, **apports** are associated with poltergeist activity.

So besides the female spirit who hovers through the house and the child who pushes the bed and plays with a white ball, who else hangs out at the old sportsman's club? Why, the former club members, most likely. C. J. tells me that when they first moved into the home, it would never stay warm. The wood stoves were removed before the home was purchased. A small fireplace in the front area of the home helped keep them warm during the winter and, since the house was large and difficult to heat, the doors to rooms rarely used were kept closed. So the first winter they lived in the two rooms near the front of the house. C. J. says that throughout the entire first

Ghostly sounds of tinkling glasses, Big Band music, and other party noises are heard in the living room of this house on Hancock.

winter she could hear the sounds of a party in the two main rooms, which are separated by an ornate wooden arch. She would get the image of scotch being poured, and would hear people talking and laughing, the sounds of glasses clinking, and people milling around near the fireplace.

"And the music," says C. J. "It would keep me up all night." She says the party noises were accompanied by the scratchy, tinny, Victrola-type sound of 1940s music from the Big Band era. C. J. says that it seemed for a while that, "There was always a party."

When I asked C. J. if her husband has witnessed anything, she says that he sees and hears nothing out of the ordinary, though he believes her. He's actually disappointed that he has not encountered anything because he does have an interest in strange phenomena.

The couple enjoy having friends over and devote every Friday evening to a gathering for board games and socializing. Most of their friends know about some of the odd happenings at the house, but none of them have ever volunteered to stay the night…except one—a true skeptic who believes that anything paranormal is hogwash. The skeptic kindly offered to housesit for them when the family took a trip. He ended up calling them the first night, saying, "I can't stay here. There are shadows moving across the walls, and I can hear people walking up and down the stairs and through the hallway."

One man who was far from being a skeptic recalls a couple of incidents that happened on a regular basis. The couple hired the man to replace the roof on the house—he knew the house well and lived there for a short time, back when Charlie owned it. He asked C. J., "So, have you tripped at the top of the stairs yet?" The man's comment confirmed what she had suspected for a long time. At first, she assumed that she was simply not watching where she was going. Then she would look down at the floor near the top of the stairs for a loose nail or some object that caused her to trip—that section of the stairs leads away from a room that C. J. and her husband refer to as the tundra, due to its constant climate.

The room in the back is, as C. J. explains, like an icebox. So cold, in fact, that she and her husband used to store soda pop in there, and even during the summer months, the soda pop would stay cold. In response to the roofer's question, C. J. said, "It's funny you should say that, because I am always tripping when I leave that room and turn to go down the stairs." The roofer responded, "Yeah. It's the ghost guy who lives in the back room. He trips people when they turn to go down the stairs." So Charlie, the former owner, must have been aware of the ghosts. A renter Charlie took in once occupied the back room the roofer refers to, the tundra room, many years ago. Whether or not the man died there or somewhere else is unknown, but years later, when the roofer lived in the home, Charlie told him not to pay much attention to any of the strange happenings upstairs. Charlie, referring to the former renter, told the roofer, "He stays in the back room."

For years, at least until C. J. and her husband moved in, no one ever touched the back room. The roofer also mentioned that when he stayed in the house, Charlie constantly had problems with the radio. Whenever he was making renovations, he always had the radio playing. "The radio," he told C. J., "would suddenly change stations to one particular station and remain there. He would switch it back, and sooner or later it would change again."

The eerie feeling associated with the back room and the top of the staircase was not enough to keep C. J. and her husband from taking matters into their own hands when it came to the room's appearance. The ceiling and walls were beginning to show signs of water damage and neglect. A complete renovation was in order. That's when the activity increased. It began with the lights turning themselves off and on in the room. One evening, the two of them were painting and doing cosmetic work in the room. After a long night of painting, cleaning, and the lights going off and on, the two went downstairs. No sooner had they arrived downstairs, when the sound of footsteps were heard overhead. "Were the kids upstairs?" thought C. J. She states that she realized that it couldn't have been the kids. They were fast asleep. Not only that, but the footsteps were heavy, like those of a man, pacing back and forth.

The house has been fairly peaceful for the last couple of years. The hovering woman has not hovered in quite a few years. No little hands have shoved the mattress upon which C. J. sleeps, and the bouncing white ball has not reappeared. C. J. and her family like it that way. But once in while, someone will still trip near the top step of the stairway. Occasionally, the sound of footsteps can be heard upstairs, with no real explanation. And every so often, party goers from another place and time seem to invite themselves over for the sound of Big Band music, some fine scotch, and plenty of conversation at the old sportsman's club.

Nancy Whiskey

Firmly planted in Corktown on Harrison Street, just a fly ball distance from the old ball field once known as Tiger Stadium, sits a wonderful pub called Nancy Whiskey. Built in 1898, it was originally a general store and a barbershop. Within four years, it became the Harrison Grill, and holds one of the earliest known liquor licenses in the state, issued in 1902. The building changed hands twice after that. A large family owned it for several years, living upstairs from the bar. It changed hands twice more before taking on its current name in the 1970s. And under a full moon on an April night, Nancy Whiskey, festooned in its Irish décor, beckoned a paranormal investigative group to come forward.

Keith, Randy, Lisa, John, and I are members of Michigan Research and Investigations of the Paranormal, and we sat at the bar with the owners, Gerald and Eva, to gather some history of the bar and listen to their accounts of what has been happening regarding the unexplained. We listened to their stories about the colorful characters that have crossed its threshold, including frequent visits by the notorious and legendary former Teamster's President, Jimmy Hoffa. According to Gerald and Eva, the regular customers have come to accept the paranormal happenings as part of the charm of Nancy Whiskey. Old ghosts were sure to make an appearance. It was going to be a long night.

The team set out to find out who was hanging out at Nancy Whiskey, a place that soon proved to be a place where everyone knows your name—and one of the past owners made certain of that. Oh, let me explain. It wasn't that he was actually with us...*let's just say he was there in spirit*. And the spirits flow freely at Nancy Whiskey, along with the warmth and camaraderie that envelops you the moment you walk in.

Eva states that her experiences mostly involve the doors opening and closing on their own and the unshakeable feeling of being watched. She was cleaning in the kitchen near the grill one afternoon, and it was very warm. She turned off the vent and felt somebody watching her. She states that it suddenly turned icy cold. Eva thought that, due to the temperature change, maybe Gerald had gone to get a fan. But Eva was alone in the kitchen and there was no fan in sight. When I asked Eva and Gerald if anything unusual happened in the kitchen that might possibly point to a connection with a spirit visitor, they told me about a fire there in 2000, which led to an interesting discovery. Now, the discovery led to spirits all right, but the drinking kind! At the time, the building was owned by Nancy McNiven, who ran the business for more than a decade before selling it to Eva and Gerald. The fire began on the stove and that part of the kitchen was gutted and rebuilt.

As most paranormal investigators are aware, renovations often stir up ghosts, secrets, and bits of history. When the remodeling took place after the fire, the construction workers pulled out the old stove to replace it. Behind it was a trap door with a hidden set of stairs leading to the basement. At the bottom of those stairs was a wooden wall and behind that wall was an old still. The only access to it was from the kitchen. Gerald and Eva mention that Nancy was surprised that there was ever a trap door at all. Nancy lived across the street from the place and thought she knew the history quite well. They mention that Nancy had no idea that business was booming during Prohibition. Having a liquor license since 1902 is a testament somehow to keeping the watering hole wet and Gerald probably speaks for all of the past owners when he mentions that even during the dry years, people would be crazy to think it would stop just because the Feds were sniffing around the joint. But "Harrison's," as it was called back then, appeared to the Feds as a nice, wholesome restaurant. Too bad for the Feds—they didn't bother to check what was being served behind the stove. Gerald proudly sums up his tongue-in-cheek motto of the centuries-old business by saying, "Hey—we never stopped serving."

Gerald and Eva mention that their nerves were rattled late one evening when just the two of them were alone in the building. Their quiet night was interrupted by the front door, which opened by itself and, with alarming force, slammed shut. It wouldn't be unusual, given that doors sometimes do that. However, all of the doors were shut and *locked* tight, since they were not open for business that evening. The couple also states that doors that are supposed to be left open are often discovered closed. The odd activity is aimed at other family members, as well. Gerald's sister, the manager of Nancy Whiskey, sometimes hears hushed conversations taking place in the bathroom when no one else is in the building.

In addition to doors opening and closing, the feeling of being watched, and the severe temperature changes, the most prominent display of activity is centered around the bar itself. Eva tells me that for a period of time, there was a constant issue with wine glasses dropping. The wine glasses are suspended from an upper rack at the bar. On a regular basis, the wine glasses would slide out and come crashing down—when none of the staff was anywhere near the wine glass racks. To prevent breakage, Eva finally had to put rubber stoppers at the edge of the wine glass holders. Eva will not tolerate backlash from the spirits and will tell them she does not approve of that kind of behavior.

Even more bizarre is the row of shot glasses on the bar that slide around and get knocked over for no apparent reason. Gerald says the shot glasses are lined up neatly by closing time. The next morning, he'll find them askew. But the true test of nerves is to witness what Gerald has when it comes to the bottles of liquor. The bottles are lined up side by side on the bar. A bottle or two will sometimes routinely slide forward and then slam, face down, onto the bar. Gerald is convinced that the culprit is... "A belligerent Irishman named Owen."

Owen died at age 69 and owned the bar before Nancy McNiven became the proprietor after his death. Nancy, an Irish beauty born and raised in southwest Detroit, was the long-time ladylove of Owen. Although they never married, the two were together for many years—both of their photos hang prominently from the bar—Owen's photo on the right, Nancy's to the left. It's interesting to note that the shot glasses and the bottles that slam forward are underneath Owen's photo. Owen and Nancy met in the late 1930s and spent many years together. Gerald's family knew Owen well, and Gerald recalls his childhood years when Owen ran nearby McCarthy's bar on Fort Street at Trumbull, eventually acquiring Nancy Whiskey. He tells me that Owen never liked him very much, and profanity was part of his everyday vocabulary. "He didn't like anybody," laughs Gerald.

Besides the fact that Nancy was the name of Owen's lady, Nancy Whiskey is also the name of Owen's favorite ballad, which tells the story of a weaver who proclaims his love for whiskey. Gerald believes that the unexplained activity is just Owen saying, "I'm still here."

Nancy Whiskey bar—viewed from "Owen's bar stool." The former owner's restless spirit is appeased when his favorite drink is set on the bar.

A barmaid who knew Owen for twenty-five years echoes the statement. The barmaid, on occasion, would be in the basement and would hear footsteps and banging noises upstairs. Again, when the building was locked down for the night. Eva and Gerald tell me that the barmaid is one who is 'not easily rattled' and knows that it's only Owen, trying to get her attention. She recently told Eva, "I haven't poured Owen a drink in a long time. But today I poured him one. It was the only way for me to be able to get anything done around here." When the barmaid experiences doors that suddenly close on their own, when she hears footsteps, or feels that she's being watched, she simply pours a glass of Jameson's whiskey with water—Owen's favorite drink—and sets it on the bar in front of 'his' chair. The unexplained activity ceases, for a while. I think the barmaid is one smart lady. The fact that she knew Owen for so many years and has picked up on the fact that maybe he needed a good, stiff drink, and supplied it for him, is one way to bring about some peace and quiet when there's work to be done. Many cultures have practiced this simple ritual for centuries. It's widely accepted among those who research and experience activity of this nature that often, the spirits can be appeased with a favorite food, beverage, or other type of tangible good that they were connected with when they were here on Earth. As I sat listening to Gerald, I had to interject when he started talking about Owen. I felt the chair I was sitting in get extremely hot, and I started getting heart palpitations. Lisa, who was seated next to me, also started to feel similar sensations.

"I know this is probably going to sound strange," I told Gerald, "but I have to go with my gut instinct on this...did Owen have some sort of heart condition?" "Yes, he did," replied Gerald. "He died of a heart attack. In fact, right now you are sitting in *his* chair." Maybe Owen was there, maybe not. But there is firm agreement among the staff that, at one time or another, there is definitely something going on after hours.

One of the most fascinating pieces of history Gerald and Eva told us about was "Jimmy's Booth." An old wooden phone booth, partially intact, still remains on the main floor, and has been there since the 1940s. Why is it referred to as "Jimmy's Booth?" Because the phone booth was often used on a regular basis by the notorious Union leader, James R. Hoffa, former president of the Teamsters Union Local 299. The union hall is located three short blocks from Nancy Whiskey. As Hoffa became a full-time union organizer for the International Brotherhood of Teamsters in the 1940s, he would come into the bar on a daily basis. Gerald states that the phone booth was the closest public phone available nearest the union hall that offered at least some bit of privacy. Hoffa, who was not a drinker, used to run over during lunch breaks to make his calls from the phone booth. Later, when he became the union president in 1957, the bar kept the phone booth, but instead of standing and talking, they honored Hoffa with his own private phone hidden behind the bar, so that he could sit, enjoy a soft drink, and make and receive calls.

Gerald states, "The bar had two phones—one for the business, and one for Hoffa." The personal Hoffa phone was held inside a wooden box and was placed in a secured area behind the bar. Hoffa would come in and sit at the first barstool in the corner. "That was Jimmy's seat," says Gerald. "Whoever was working behind the bar would slide the phone out and immediately set it down at the bar in front of Jimmy. Nobody ever touched that phone except Hoffa."

Some scenes from the 1992 film, "Hoffa," were filmed at Nancy Whiskey and actor Jack Nicholson, who played the title role, would hang out at the bar when production had stopped for the day. I took a couple of photos of the phone booth later that evening, and asked Mr. Hoffa to make an appearance. Unfortunately, I did not capture anything even remotely paranormal, though a unique-looking orb showed up about five and half feet from the floor at the side of the phone booth. No concrete evidence, so to speak, but the orb is kind of odd.

Gerald and Eva completed giving us the history of the building and sharing their experiences with us, and Gerald wrapped up by giving the team a tour of the main floor, the basement, and the upper floor, which houses a private bar and a small apartment. Randy and I began filming in the basement and attempted to capture spirit voices on our recorders. John, Lisa, and Keith remained on the main floor and took photos in the bar. We then switched areas, and completed the investigation with the entire group together, upstairs. Randy began filming as he and I descended the stairs into the basement. The moment we got downstairs, which took thirteen seconds, his video camera shut down, even though the battery had just been charged. The camera started up again after thirteen seconds. Again, thirteen seconds later, it shut down. I did not get any voices on the recorder, but I did get touched on the forehead, and then the back of my head was lightly stroked. Randy and I then went to the main floor to join Keith, while Lisa and John headed downstairs.

Besides a few orbs, which can often be easily explained away, we captured a head and shoulders shot of a man in a mirror, though the image is difficult to make out unless you really look for it, again nothing concrete. A couple of strange sounds on the voice recorder came out fairly clearly. During the middle of the investigation, I sat at the bar. All was quiet. I began to record using an extended microphone. Most often, when you're trying to capture electronic voice phenomena, nothing is heard when you go "live," that is, when you are asking the spirit questions. It's usually only during playback that the voice can be heard, if at all. I recommend stereo headsets when playing back your recordings—it assists in letting you hear distinct sounds or voices you may not otherwise hear. In any case, I sat at the bar and began to ask if anyone was behind the bar. I then said, "Can you tell me your name?" When I played the recorder the following morning, there is a two-second hesitation after my question, and then in a far-away male voice, "OWEN!" is heard. It was said with such annoyance I nearly jumped out of my chair when I heard it.

Out of all the various types of possible connection with phenomena—whether it be mists, lights, apparitions, orbs, knockings, or any number of alleged signs—my favorite is **electronic voice phenomena, or EVP**. It is difficult to be absolutely certain that a true spirit voice is captured, and it is extremely easy to debunk. Whispers from other investigators, fans or other electrical devices, equipment noises, airplanes flying overhead, and hundreds of other possibilities can instantly debunk a spirit voice—unless the voice is extremely clear and there is very little room for argument over what was said.

Take for example the following scenario:

Toward the end of the investigation, the team agreed to wrap things up. I had shut off my recorder and one of the team members said, "It's time to go." Seconds later a loud grunt is heard. None of the investigators made the noise. Lisa captured it quite nicely, however the window was open and it could have been someone down the street, below the building, making the noise. I still believe Lisa captured an annoying "harrumph" from an unknown source, but everything must be taken into consideration and natural occurrences have to be ruled out—in this case, an open window may have allowed street noises to be carried upstairs where we were recording.

The band, the Copycats, pose with friends after performing at Nancy Whiskey. Though cigarette smoke has been ruled out, the unidentified white streaks remain a mystery. *Courtesy of the Copycats*

We were really hoping to capture something upstairs because Gerald told us that a couple of years ago, he and a worker were doing some construction and renovation up there and an odd incident occurred. Gerald, unknown to the worker, had gone downstairs to retrieve a tool. As he returned and approached the top of the stairs, the fellow worker swung around, wild-eyed, and asked, "What are you doing over there? You are in the bathroom!" Gerald said, "No. I've been downstairs." The worker asked, "Who else is here?" "Nobody," replied Gerald, "It's just us two." The worker asked, "Well then **WHO** is in the bathroom?" Apparently, the worker saw, out of the corner of his eye, a male figure walk around the corner, enter the bathroom, and shut the door behind him.

Sometimes, it is not just the paranormal investigators who capture the unexplained on film, on a voice recorder, or with a video camera. Take, for example, the photo I received from Eva after the investigation. A local band, the Copycats, musicians who appear on a fairly regular basis at Nancy Whiskey, posed for a photo after "Parade Day," the busiest and most important day of the year for those who visit Nancy Whiskey. Parade Day is when the annual St. Patrick's Day parade in Detroit takes place, and after the parade the bar is packed with revelers, singers, and partygoers. A photo sent to me by Eva shows the band goofing around and obviously having a great time, and directly behind them is a strange mist. There was no cigarette smoke behind them, they were against a wall, and the mist seems to shoot out in streaks and then break into odd formations. Because the investigative team was not there when the photo was taken, it's difficult to determine whether or not the mist can be explained by natural causes. I thought the photo was interesting, however, and have included it here.

The deciding factor in whether or not paranormal activity had been truly captured or recorded during an investigation is most often left to chance. In exterior photos, even the slightest bit of rain or snow can automatically debunk orbs, streaks, lights, and other anomalies. The chance that the spirits just don't feel like playing that day can leave an investigator disappointed. Out of the many investigations performed throughout any given time frame, the chance of actually capturing true phenomena on film is scant. That is why I always appreciate it when the spirits come through for me. I often thank them when I'm attempting to capture EVP, even if I don't hear the recording until I've returned home and have gone through the evidence.

And because Owen called out to me from the bar and left his faint, but stern introduction on my voice recorder, I pay respects here to the man who was known as a mean old Irishman who loved his whiskey. After all, he did come through for me when I introduced myself and asked who was behind the bar that night.

We may never know why Owen pays regular visits. Why the doors slam shut when they're open. Or remain open when they're supposed to be closed. Or why the shot glasses move around, the wine glasses slip from their racks, or bottles periodically slam face down on their own. Perhaps it's his Irish temperament or his need to let people know that he's still there to oversee the day-to-day operations. So I leave you with Owen's song. It's best sung with a whiskey in one hand and a friend on either side of you, on a bar stool, at a place in Corktown called Nancy Whiskey.

The song tells the story of a hard-working man who happens to catch the scent of whiskey at a nearby pub, gets drawn in, and spends eternity professing his love for the amber liquid. The partial lyrics to Owen's favorite ode to the drink go something like this:

I'm a weaver, a Carlton weaver, I'm a rash and a roving blade
I've got silver in my pockets and I follow the roving trade
Whiskey, Whiskey, Nancy Whiskey
Whiskey, Whiskey, Nancy-O
As I went down through Glasgow City,
Nancy Whiskey I chanced to smell
I went in, sat down beside her, seven long years I loved her well
Whiskey, Whiskey, Nancy Whiskey
 Whiskey, Whiskey, Nancy-O
So come all you weavers, you Carlton weavers, come all
        you weavers, where e'er you be
Beware of Whiskey, Nancy Whiskey, she'll ruin you
        like she ruined me

(Original title: "Long Cookstown", from *Sam Henry's Songs of the People, 1923-1939*.
The National Library of Ireland, Dublin.)

From the bullet holes that still remain in the walls from a forgotten shootout of long ago, to the original tin ceiling and the beautiful woodwork, to the photos of Owen and Nancy taken during a bygone era, Nancy Whiskey stands as a tribute to those colorful characters who have entered through its doors from the past couple of centuries. It holds fond memories of the customers who still enjoy a shot and a beer after the annual St. Patrick's Day parade. It retains those memories of customers in the 1950s that celebrated after watching third basemen George Kell in action after another game at the old ballpark nearby. It still holds, partially intact, the wooden phone booth affectionately called "Jimmy's Booth," named after the notorious Union leader, James R. Hoffa, whose disappearance is still one of the great mysteries connected to the city of Detroit. Bands like the Copycats still rock the house, the drinks are lined up, and the grill is hot. Nancy Whiskey is the kind of place that welcomes all who enter...*and maybe some who never really left.*

2

Etta Wriedt

Detroit's Direct-Voice Medium

---

*"I am silent on the subject of the afterlife because of necessity.
I have friends in both places."*

-- Will Clemens,
Mark Twain, His Life and Work

Few Detroiters are aware of a medium from the Motor City who was held in high regard in the early 1900s among spiritualists, authors, statesmen, and the former prime minister of Canada, to name a few. Add to that a popular British newspaper editor who befriended this medium during her lifetime, and eventually came back to visit in spirit form after a national tragedy.

Etta Wriedt was born in Detroit in 1859, leading a quiet life until her gift of communicating with the dead began to surface when she was in her thirties. By her mid-fifties, Wriedt became famous for her ability to speak to the dead and was known as a direct-voice medium. **Direct-voice mediums** differ from channelers, or those who go into a trance. Rather, the direct-voice medium speaks in their own voice and can hold conversations with spirits, sometimes two or three simultaneously. In some cases, the spirit speaks directly to those at the sitting and the direct-voice medium may not even hear the spirit speak.

Wriedt was known to hold hundreds of séances, and to assist in bringing forth spirits who were connected to those who attended her sittings, or séances. Usually relatives or spirit guides of those in attendance would manifest, and detailed documentation notes that many of the spirits materialized to the point that they were often seen in solid form. Sometimes, only a hand or an arm would materialize, and often, those who sat in a circle would receive messages whispered in their ear. Spirits who spoke Arabic, Croatian, Serbian, Dutch, French, German, Hebrew, Hindustani, Spanish, Italian, Norwegian, Welsh, Scotch, and Gaelic came through during the many years Wriedt held séances, though she only spoke English throughout her lifetime.

Wriedt also succeeded in communicating with the spirits through the use of a widely popular device in the early 1900s called a **spirit trumpet**, or simply, a trumpet. *A trumpet is a conical shaped device that is made from cardboard, paper, tin, or aluminum. Often, a spirit's voice may be too weak to be heard aloud, and the principle use of the trumpet is to act as a megaphone to increase the sound of the voice so that it can be heard during the séance.* Wriedt would clairvoyantly read names that were shown to her by the spirits. She then called the name aloud, and if the name was recognized by any of the sitters, the communication would commence. If the name was not recognized, the spirit was "cleared out," to avoid making contact with spirits whose intent was hostile or malevolent. Often, she held sittings in the daylight, which most mediums would never do. Wriedt's heyday was during the peak of the Spiritualism movement.

The rise of Spiritualism brought about an interest in séances, where groups would gather in the parlor to make contact with the dead. Spiritualism's popularity surfaced in 1848, when the Fox sisters – Kate, Maggie, and Leah – began hearing **rappings** during séances. Except for a handful of clustered groups in Cassadaga, Florida, parts of Massachusetts, California, and throughout Lily Dale, New York, the research, development, and scientific studies in the field of parapsychology was more advanced and widely accepted in the United Kingdom than in the United States. It was fashionable in Britain for the middle- and upper-class to hold tea and séances and, in its infancy, Spiritualism was just as much a well-to-do social gathering as it was spiritual. When scientific researchers and prominent figures began to take note, its curiosity piqued the interest of the mass public.

Its popularity in the United States became heightened, due in part to Civil War widows seeking solace in the reassurance that their loved ones could return in spirit with a message or two. The movement gave the green light to those with psychic gifts and those with a keen interest in life after death communication to form Spiritualist camps.

Spiritualism was not without tricksters and frauds, especially among the middle and lower classes, whose reputations were less at stake than those in the upper-class. Several self-appointed mediums used every trick imaginable to reap monetary gain from believers, the hopeful, and the curious.

It was during this time period that spirit photography emerged. Although it can be argued that some of the evidence was quite compelling, most of it was simply a way for tricksters to prey on those who lost a loved one and felt an emotional pull to somehow have the deceased appear with them in a photo. Photographers would superimpose photos on images of a subject. While the subject was sitting for the photo, the photographer would insert a glass plate with a photo previously taken of a loved one—or chosen from a stock of photos the photographer kept under wraps. The results, to the untrained eye, were amazing. Of course, the person who sat for the photo was vulnerable and so overwrought that he or she was willing to believe that their loved one on the other side materialized somehow and sat with them during the photo session.

Spiritualism was also fueled in part by its acceptance and practices by Mary Todd Lincoln and the Fox sisters in the United States and, in the United Kingdom, by such notorious figures as the British Naval Vice Admiral Usborne Moore, Sir Arthur Conan Doyle, and W. T. "William" Stead, a well-known journalist, peace activist, and newspaper editor. In fact, it was by the support and invitation of Stead, that the 51-year-old Wriedt made her Atlantic crossing—leaving her home in Detroit in 1911 for the United Kingdom—to hold the first of many séances recorded by Stead's secretary.

When word spread to the United Kingdom about the "direct-voice medium from Detroit," Stead arranged for Wriedt to arrive via steamship. At the time, Detroit was experiencing its industrial boom, and little attention was paid to those who had a penchant for speaking to the spirits. It is said that Wriedt was the proof of her own genuineness. To give away her gift and not charge would be to minimize her gift of mediumship. To charge exorbitant fees would label her a charlatan. Therefore, Wriedt always asked for the simple fee of one dollar, whether holding séances in small apartments with mere acquaintances and friends, or in exquisite parlors with the crown heads of Europe. Her sittings, arranged by Stead in 1911, met with much acclaim, and she was invited to return again in 1912 and 1913. This time Vice Admiral Usborne Moore arranged her overseas travel. In both 1915 and 1919, she traveled abroad again by the invitation of Moore, mostly holding séances in Rothesay, Scotland.

By this time, Wriedt's sittings were recorded and analyzed, and a small, dedicated group of sitters regularly gathered to hear messages from the afterlife. Along with W. T. Stead, Admiral Moore, Sir Arthur Conan Doyle, and other reputable persons, psychical researcher William F. Barrett attended the sittings and noted details about the experiences. During one particular séance, the spirit of Professor Henry Sidgwick came through with the assistance of Wriedt. Barrett was familiar with Sidgwick through his work as a member of the Metaphysical Society and as the first president and a founder of the Society for Psychical Research. Much of Sidgwick's work, prior to his passing in 1900, was devoted to promoting the higher education of women. Barrett recalls the moment he realized that the spirit communicating with the group that evening was indeed Henry Sidgwick by what was said by Sidgwick himself.

Barrett states, "Mrs. Wriedt doubtless had heard his name, but he died before she visited England, and I doubt if she, or many others who knew him by name, were aware that he stammered badly. So I asked the voice 'Are you all right now?' not referring to his stammering. Immediately the voice replied 'You mean the impediment in my speech, but I do not stutter now' ... I went to Mrs. Wriedt's séances in a somewhat skeptical spirit, but I came to the conclusion that she is a genuine and remarkable medium, and has given abundant proof to others besides myself that the voices and the contents of the messages given are wholly beyond the range of trickery or collusion."

Other features of Wriedt's séances included flowers being taken from vases and placed in the hands of sitters in the dark in different parts of the room. Some sitters described invisible fingers touching them and raps that were heard on the trumpet, in an attempt to urge a hesitating person in the room to answer promptly when spoken to.

Wriedt traveled between the United Kingdom and Detroit a total of five times, and was visited in Detroit by those within her circle of friends and colleagues, including Vice Admiral Moore and, years later, by W. L. Mackenzie King, the former prime minister of Canada, with whom she would spend a great deal of time toward the end of her lifetime. Wriedt was not fond of notoriety, and preferred to simply remain out of the public eye. It was said that, regarding the media, Wriedt felt that those in the media would simply write what they wanted anyhow, and it was of no use to her what they believed.

In *The Voices, A Sequel to Glimpses of the Next State*, Vice Admiral Moore describes Wriedt: "Mrs. Wriedt does not permit herself to be investigated by merely curious people, or those who are known to be out simply in search of fraud; who, in short, have no constructive purpose in view. She says she went through all this a quarter of a century ago, and that it is not reasonable to expect her to start her mission in every town by being gagged, tied up, and physically tested by strangers, some of whom may be entirely ignorant of the business in hand. If the evidence of identity which come out in such profusion during her séances do not appeal to those who hear them, she is content to let the sitters think what they like. She has no objection whatever to the really open-minded skeptic."

Sir Arthur Conan Doyle, best known for penning the Sherlock Holmes mysteries, was a great believer in the authenticity of Wriedt's mediumship. In his book, *The History of Spiritualism, Volume II*, Doyle writes, "The reality of her powers may best be judged by a short description of results...at the evening sitting, a succession of friends came through with every possible sign of their identity. One sitter was approached by her father, recently dead, who began by the hard, dry cough which had appeared in his last illness."

He also documents a sitter who seemed to be skeptical at first, about a visit from a relative from the other side, during one of Wriedt's sessions. Doyle states, "Another sitter had a visit from one who claimed to be his grand-aunt. The relationship was denied, but on inquiry at home it was found that he had actually had an aunt of that name who died in his childhood. Telepathy has to be strained very far to cover such cases."

Wriedt's friend and supporter, William Stead, was scheduled to attend a conference in New York in April of 1912. Wriedt reportedly was to accompany him on his return voyage to Southampton from New York, for her second visit to once again hold sittings in England. However, a strange turn of events, to say the least, would prevent Stead from seeing those plans through. Stead had been invited by then-U.S. President, William Howard Taft, to take part in a peace congress at Carnegie Hall in New York. Stead boarded the vessel in Southampton, England, headed for America. He held quite an interest in steamships, and had taken great care to see to the details of Wriedt's steamship crossing to Southampton the year prior.

This was at a time when ship-building was all the rage. Years earlier Stead, in 1886, had written a well-received article entitled, "How the Steamship Went Down in Mid-Atlantic...by a Survivor." The "worst-case scenario" article was written to call attention to the need to ensure that there were always sufficient lifeboats on luxury ocean liners, in case of disaster. Then, in 1892, Stead wrote a series of stories for his novel, *From the Old World to the New*, in which he included a story about a ship that collided with an iceberg.

Some say that Stead, a firm believer in communication between the dead and the living, predicted his own demise. Others say it was simply a coincidence. The vessel he boarded on that spring day in April 1912, by invitation of President Taft, was a brand new ship on its maiden voyage, and Stead had a first-class ticket. The name of the ship was the RMS Titanic.

Survivors on the ship would later recall seeing Stead, after the ship hit the iceberg, leaving the first-class section to assist women and children into the lifeboats. Another survivor witnessed Stead holding back men who attempted to board the lifeboats ahead of the women and children. He was also remembered as holding deep conversations about spiritual matters at mealtime, while aboard the fateful voyage.

Over seventy reports of Stead making contact with family members and those within his circle of friends in the study of Spiritualism, including Sir Arthur Conan Doyle and Etta Wriedt, have been carefully recorded and noted, most especially by the assistance of Stead's daughter Estelle. Wriedt gave a sitting in Wimbledon, attended by Admiral Moore and Stead's daughter, Estelle. Moore later documented that Stead came through and gave details to his daughter about his final moments aboard the Titanic. Contrary to reports that he had been last seen clinging to a raft with his feet frozen until he lost his grip, Stead—whose body was never recovered—relayed detailed messages throughout several séances, within the months following his demise.

At a small, private sitting in the home of an acquaintance, Wriedt held a sitting where Stead's voice came through. "I am so happy to be with you again," his voice said. He informed his daughter that he was struck on the head, prior to hitting the water, which prevented him from feeling the actual sensation of drowning. He also stated that there were several hundred souls that hovered over their floating bodies, and that some who perished could not fully comprehend their new state of being. Further messages came through where Stead says, "After what felt like a few minutes, they [the bodies in the water] all seemed to rise vertically into the air at a terrific speed. "I cannot tell how long our journey lasted, nor how far from the earth we were when arrived, but it was a gloriously beautiful arrival. It was like walking from your own English winter gloom into the radiance of an Indian sky. There, all was brightness and beauty."

On the subject of the attempt to communicate with mediums, Stead revealed that there were souls in the afterlife with him who had the power of sensing mediums on the earth who could be used for communication. One soul in particular had assisted him in learning to materialize, since he seemed to only be able to get his face to materialize, nothing more. He stated, during one séance, that a strong soul that was with him on the other side said he should imagine he was there, standing among the living, with a strong light thrown upon himself. Stead also revealed during a sitting that he should will himself to appear nearest the most sensitive person there, concentrate on a short sentence, and repeat it with much emphasis until he could hear it being spoken. Stead's message was that he should, "...hold the visualization very deliberately and in detail, and keep it fixed upon my mind, that at that moment I was there and they were conscious of it."

By the 1930s, Wriedt was nearing her golden years, and spent the remainder of her life holding séances and readings closer to home in Detroit, although she traveled often to nearby Canada, mainly to visit with Mackenzie King, the former prime minister of Canada.

Mackenzie King accomplished a great deal during his political career, most notably as Canada's prime minister, covering three terms in a span of twenty-two years. It wasn't until after his death in 1950 that his private life was revealed to be in stark contrast to the image he portrayed to the public. Through detailed diaries, King revealed his interest in contacting the spirits of the dead, most especially after losing several family members and a close friend within a short period of time during and just after World War I. He gave specific instructions to his butler that, upon his death, the diaries were to be burned. His final wishes were never carried out and the personal memoirs are filed with the National Archives of Canada.

The former prime minister was enthralled by dream interpretation, table rappings, and numerology. He spent many days and nights holding sittings where he spoke with his deceased mother, brother, and grandfather, and had come to rely on Wriedt as a regular method of communication with the dead. A neighbor and friend, Joan Patteson, attended séances with him and shared many long walks discussing parapsychology along King's estate at Kingsmere, in Quebec, where Patteson and her husband rented a cottage. Joan Patteson was mentioned often in the diaries, as was Etta Wriedt.

King began consulting with a variety of mediums, beginning in 1920, though he considered Wriedt to be his favorite, often making several visits to Detroit over a ten-year time span. Wriedt paid several visits to Ottawa, and visited with King and Joan Patteson in Kingsmere, discussing table rappings, messages received from deceased politicians, and other paranormal phenomena. Wriedt and the former prime minister kept in contact throughout the next few years until her death at age eighty-three on September 13, 1942.

Very few public photos or quotes are available to more deeply reveal the personality and to better understand the woman who was Etta Wriedt. The connections she made with famous leaders, politicians, and public figures spanned across two continents for more than four decades. When asked to supply a photo of herself and a short biography to be included in the book, *Dawn of the Awakened Mind*, published in 1920, Wriedt responded with a note to the author which read, "I never had a photo taken since I was a little girl; and as to my life being printed, I don't really care for it. Let people remember me as they knew me." Some mediums and psychics are buoyed by notoriety and an ego-induced desire to believe that psychic ability is equated with wisdom and superiority.

Etta Wriedt, Detroit's Spiritualist medium, poses in this 1934 photo taken on the property of the former Prime Minister of Canada.
Courtesy of the Library and Archives Canada, Copy Number PA178407.

Others, such as Etta Wriedt, do what they are put on this earth to do, complete their life's mission and cross over without fanfare. Wriedt understood her gift of mediumship was simply an instrument, in which to further the advancement of understanding the link between the here and now, and what lies beyond in the afterlife.

3

Spirits Served Here

"You can tell a ghost to leave and it usually will at the time.
But unless you find out why it haunts and help it solve its problem,
it will return sooner or later."

-- Marion Kuclo (Gundella),
Michigan Haunts & Hauntings

The three-bedroom home near Cadieux Road and East Warren Avenue sat far back on a corner lot. Because it stood at the end of the block, it had only one set of next-door neighbors, to the east. The side of the home facing west overlooked an alley, and this alley separated the dwelling from a small row of businesses and busy East Warren Avenue. For many years, the large front yard held two peach trees and a large row of currant bushes. The same family occupied the home for nearly fifty years, and their two daughters still remember how the house seemed to *come alive* when the sun went down.

During the 1970s, the girls were in their teens and there were at least two spirits roaming the house. One, for certain, was their grandfather, who passed away in 1972. The older daughter, Anne, recalls the night he passed away. She was half asleep and was awakened by her grandfather standing over her. He leaned down and kissed her on the forehead. She still remembers the way his whiskers scratched her forehead. On the first anniversary of his passing, she was alone in the living room, watching television, and remembers feeling a presence watching her. She still recalls the details of the olive-green 1970s swivel chair where the presence was felt. The chair began rocking back and forth by itself. Anne remembers the rocking continued for several minutes when it stopped suddenly. She heard the sound of someone, full weight, getting out of the heavy vinyl chair. She believes it was her grandfather who, she recalls, had purchased the television for her family just before he died. "Grandpa loved television. He just thought it was the greatest invention," she says, laughing. Years later, on Christmas Day, she saw his smiling reflection in a bedroom mirror. Christmas Day was especially connected with their grandfather, since it was also his birthday.

Grandfather, who was a carpenter, was always warning the kids when they were young "Don't touch that" or "Don't mess with my tools." All four of the children in the family would laugh and reminisce about grandfather's favorite saying, "Don't monkey around." At a holiday gathering several years after grandfather's passing, the younger daughter, Mary, had gone to the attic in search of an item. While searching for the item, she stumbled upon a large toolbox she recognized as her grandfather's. Mary states that she dusted off the toolbox and applied heavy force to the latch to open it, as it was jammed shut. It was then that she heard "Careful, child! Go slow. You're going to cut yourself!" It was the voice of her grandfather. Mary heeded her grandfather's words. Slowly and carefully she worked at the latch until it opened. When the overstuffed toolbox sprang open, out popped a handsaw, blade first. Had Mary continued to apply force to the latch, her fingers would have come into direct contact with the blade. Grandfather kept an eye out on the family and, from time to time, made his presence known.

But most of the unexplained activity that occurred during the 1970s, the family believes, was caused by an unruly old ghost named Arnold.

It was the height of the coming of age years for Anne and Mary, and during this time period, the ghostly activities were at their peak. *The teen years seem to be connected to atmospheric changes, kinetic energy, and transference*. And the activity in the house where Anne and Mary grew up was no different.

In particular, the doors were constantly opening and closing by themselves—especially in the bedroom they shared. The older daughter, Anne, recalls standing near the bedroom doorway and telling her sister, "I am going to ask the ghost what his name is." Instantly, a name that sounded like "Arnold" popped into her head. So there it was. From now on, the ghost was addressed by his name. Although never harmful or vicious, Arnold was a bit of a prankster and would sometimes just do things to let the girls know he was there. Even their two brothers would get in on the phenomenon fun by blaming lost items on Arnold. Or calling out, "Arnold's here," when they'd hear a knock or two on the back door.

"He was mostly active during the summer months," says Mary. "Especially with the doors," adds Anne. The creaking at night and doors opening and closing of their own volition were quickly explained by their mother, who would tell them it was just the house, "...settling down for the night."

Anne says, "I'm sure every young person who has spent some time in an older home has had these explanations handed down to them from their parents. "It's just your imagination...older houses make noises...it's just the wind." She adds, "What I want to know is, does the wind also shake the brass doorknobs?" That's exactly what Anne experienced while in her bedroom when she was nine years old. The girls' bedroom had a closet that, years later, revealed an interesting secret.

One evening, Anne experienced a paranormal incident that shook her to the core, and it's still imbedded in her memory some thirty-five years later.

"I was awakened by the bright moon shining through my bedroom window. Through the light coming through the window, I saw movement near the closet. The doors of the closet began to open on their own. I was terrified. All I could do was to stare at the closet doors."

Anne thought maybe her sister was playing tricks, but Mary was at a slumber party that night. After what seemed like an eternity, the doors stopped moving.

Finally, Anne fell into a deep sleep, only to awaken several hours later when she felt her bed moving. Or, rather, just the foot of the bed.

Anne was paralyzed as the foot of the bed lifted several inches into the air and, before she could even summon a scream, the bed dropped to the floor with a bang.

"It was as if someone was looking for something...going through the closet, lifting up the bed...I just couldn't figure it out."

If Arnold the ghost was looking for something, what was it? And why all the activity surrounding that particular bedroom? Perhaps a little history on the house could help solve the mystery.

The house was in close proximity to Detroit River and Lake St. Clair, and local residents often fell asleep to the sounds of foghorns as freighters passed one another along the waterway. The type of area where a lazy drive along Jefferson Avenue in the summer months or a bike ride along the pristine shoreline was the perfect way to spend a sleepy Sunday.

The quiet nights on the riverfront were not always quiet. In fact, one particular time period in Detroit's history would prove that, indeed, the rivers were much more active at night than they were during the day. The increase in nighttime activity was mainly due to the outlaw of liquor, officially declared on January 16, 1920.

According to *The Detroit News*, during Prohibition, seventy-five percent of the United States' liquor supply was illegally smuggled across these waterways. Canada, in a neighborly gesture, was more than happy to supply its high and dry U.S. friends with beer, wine, and spirits, using the Motor City as its connection. Smuggling booze across the border was an all-season sport. Winter provided the perfect opportunity for smugglers to provide their services in full view of the public. At some points along the Detroit River, only a mile or two separated the two countries, providing easy access for skaters towing large sleds filled with children or other innocent props sitting atop a case of Canadian whiskey or other spirits. And, of course, with Detroit's automobile industry in high gear, a quick trip over the ice by car was not unusual. High-paid smugglers removed the back seats and stored cases of beer or liquor inside, or attached the booze to the underbelly of the vehicle.

In fact, the rumrunners and bootleggers of the Detroit area reaped such a profit that it was second only to the auto industry in business revenues, reaching an estimated $215 million dollars in 1929. But with these elaborate schemes came a heavy price, which is why many Detroit residents figured it was cheaper to make their own booze. Speakeasies were cropping up faster than the Feds could bust 'em up. Often, homeowners secretly advertised their illegal wares by placing a stuffed tiger or pig in the window. The "blind pig," as it was coined, became a welcome sign for thirsty patrons that alcohol was available for consumption. So what does all of this have to do with Arnold, the busy ghost who always seemed to be looking for something?

As the 1970s became history and the girls graduated from high school, the family in that old Victorian home began doing some remodeling. While painting the basement walls, the girls' mother discovered a large, deep storage area that, up until now, the family had never even known existed. This storage area was directly below the girls' bedroom. Their mother yanked a few nails loose and discovered a long, deep shelf still holding its precious treasures of a bygone era—seven large whiskey jugs topped with corks and *FILLED* with homemade booze. Next to the row of glass jugs was a homemade "still" or booze-making machine. It was as if the bootlegger had a little assembly line going and simply closed up shop on a temporary basis. Whose whiskey was stored in that hidden shelf, nailed shut for nearly six decades? Could Arnold have been searching for his bootleg supplies and equipment? Were the fruit trees and berry bushes that once flourished on the property used to flavor the precious booze? Could the alley to the west of the home, once canvassed in large trees, been the perfect road for Model T's to make their way, unseen, in the midnight hours, to Arnold's blind pig?

Perhaps Arnold was the true bootlegger ghost. You see, another piece of the puzzle was gathered when the siblings reunited at the home, which is now owned by the girls' older brother. On a recent Memorial Day gathering at the home, an interesting bit of history came full circle. The girls' brother found old papers and copies of deeds to the home nestled in an attic crawlspace. He dusted it off as the siblings sat outside around the old picnic table, where the fruit trees and berry bushes once grew.

Anne and Mary perused the abstract deed to the property and recognized many names that matched several street names in the neighborhood. Most were French names; presumably descendants of the early French settlers from early days when Detroit was in its infancy and French voyageurs were a common sighting along the Detroit River and near the Grosse Pointes. Anne suggested they look up who owned the home during Prohibition. The girls gasped when they read the name of the former owner of their childhood home during the Prohibition era. The French gentleman's name was Honor, which may have sounded like "Arnold," to the girls. The girls may not have been too far off the mark when, as children, they named their busy ghost friend Arnold.

The homemade beer, wine, and bootleg equipment are long gone, and the homemade spirits may have evaporated. But for two sisters coming of age in the 1970s, there exists a certain spirit that will always remain.

4

The Candle Factory

"There are an infinite number of universes existing side by side and through which our consciousnesses constantly pass. In these universes, all possibilities exist. You are alive in some, long dead in others, and never existed in still others. Many of these ghosts could indeed be visions of people going about their business in a parallel universe or another time—or both."

-- Paul F. Eno,
Faces At the Window

The city of Ferndale is a classic midwestern town whose growth began as a community for Detroit workers during the World War I era. A small northern suburb, it borders Detroit by 8 Mile Road.

Coventry Creations, a popular supplier of "candles, oils, and spiritual goods," is situated in Ferndale's small industrial sector in the city's southeast quadrant. Founded by Jacki Smith, the company offers a full-line of metaphysical supplies, most notably, hand-poured candles designed to enhance the intentions of those who seek everything from prosperity to a happy home to attraction and more. Because of the nature of the business, Jacki believes that for some reason, she and her staff "bring it out." And Jacki has been "bringing it out" since 1992, when she made her first magical candle on her kitchen stove in Detroit. Family and friends commented on her ability to create candles for the special intentions people were seeking.

From those humble beginnings on Detroit's eastside, she launched her business, Coventry Creations, with her first line of candles, Blessed Herbal Candles. The company has since added a variety of incense, blessing kits, and essential oils. Today, along with her sister and business co-owner, Patty Shaw, Coventry has created more than twenty-five product lines that are sold through distributors all over the United States and in several foreign countries.

In February of 2008, Michigan Research and Investigations of the Paranormal was assigned to explore and assess the odd occurrences taking place at the factory. We, as investigators, try to zero in on who or what is doing the haunting. By asking specific questions, we can sometimes determine if the spirit is there because of certain people in the home or building, or if the spirit is attached to the building itself.

Jacki states that there has always been strange activity around her and the staff, dating back to the first store she had on Mack Avenue in Detroit. "The old, rickety basement in the first store," Jacki states, "was home to a blind pig during Prohibition. You can still see the benches and seating area where the people sat around drinking the illegal booze back in the 1930s." A long-time resident in the area once told Jacki that since the blind-pig business was shut down, no business had lasted more than two years. Sure enough, within two years, Jacki felt the need to move the business. First to a larger space in Clinton Township and then to a building in Highland Park that formerly housed a pawnshop which, Patty adds, "Was a creepy place. A really creepy place." Jacki finally settled the business at its current home in Ferndale, where it stands today.

So what exactly takes place behind the doors of Coventry Creations? Besides the administrative offices, the long aisles of storage for the aromatic and incense and candles, and the shipping and packaging area, the main "hub" of the site centers on the area situated in the middle of the factory, where the candles are poured.

It's possible that some of the spirits that hang out at Coventry may have been summoned, even subconsciously, by members who have attended sessions that are sometimes held in the building. Every so often, psychic readings are held there, and a group gathers to perform healings and misas to assist earth-bound spirits in finding their way back to the other side. Somewhat akin to the American form of a séance, a **misa**, or spirit circle mass, is a gathering of those who study spiritism, and like-minded individuals, led by a medium. **Spiritism** is somewhat akin to Spiritualism, though the former includes both human and animal spirit communication. The evolution of spiritism has absorbed religious practices and beliefs ranging from Santeria, Roman Catholicism, Vodou, and others. Christianity influenced many early spiritists in the Western culture, but over time spirit circles evolved and are no longer associated with one particular culture. The sessions can be focused on receiving messages from ancestors, discovering spirit guides, assisting those who are troubled by spirits around them, healing, eliminating or subsiding active hauntings, and elevating spirits to a higher plane.

But there is more activity than just what meets the eye. And it happens during the daytime as well as at night. Let's start with the shipping and packaging area. A dark shadow is sometimes seen moving around in the area. The shipping manager sees balls of light that dart back and forth along the wall. She dismisses the sunlight through the window and states that when the balls of light flicker, she checks to make sure no cars or trucks are driving past the store. The store is, in fact, on a small industrial road that sees very little public traffic.

Another staff member experienced problems with the heat gun used for shrink-wrapping packages. The employee states, "The heat gun has a real sensitive trigger. It's pretty powerful and is also very loud. For safety reasons, we unplug it when we are finished with it. One afternoon, I stopped the shrink-wrapping process since it was almost time to go home for the day. I shut off the heat gun and unplugged it. There were still several candles that needed to be wrapped however, and I guess the resident ghost was trying to tell me to get back to work. I turned my back to leave and almost jumped out of my skin. I heard the noise of the heat gun and swung around to see something very strange. The heat gun was running full force...*unplugged*!" In that same area are the shrink "sleeves" of various sizes, used to slip over the candles, which are organized in boxes by size. On several occasions, employees have come to work in the morning to find the sleeves rearranged and put in the wrong sections.

Much of the activity seems to follow Lisa, whose main responsibility is pouring the candles. As recently as one month prior to our investigation, Lisa opened the shop earlier than usual one morning. Within a few moments, she heard a set of double doors, which separates the production area from the administrative offices, opening and closing. Lisa's first thought was to call the police. "It would be at least a half hour before the rest of the staff shows up," she thought. She tiptoed toward the double doors to find no one there. Opening doors has become standard operating procedure at the shop. Even Jacki's daughter thought kindly of the spirits recently, when a closed door was opened for her before she could turn the knob. The staff finds humor in another incident centered around Lisa. At the time, Lisa had just severed ties with a love interest. Strangely enough, while rearranging the lobby, which neatly showcases each product and set, Lisa got hit with more love than she bargained for, when she got bombarded with a bottle of specially mixed essential oils

Display in the lobby of a haunted candle factory, where a bottle of essential oil blend called, "Attraction," levitated and sprayed itself on an employee.

called Attraction/Love. The bottle, which doesn't even belong on the shelf in the area she was working on, flew out of a corner as if being pushed by unseen hands. It shot through the air and pelted Lisa on her legs with such force that the bottle shattered, anointing her with the pungent aroma. No word yet on whether or not Lisa attracted any love interest, but there is something Lisa does attract and has attracted all her life—animals and animal spirits.

Wolfie

Lisa occasionally sees an apparition of a red wolf. Though some historians dispute the theory of the origin of the red wolf, it's considered to be a cross combination of the gray wolf and the coyote.

The red wolf, usually smaller in stature than other wolf species, is similar in appearance to a large fox. Lisa sees the wolf as a full-form apparition, yet he appears quite solid looking. The wolf enters and exits only through the back door of the candle factory—which is often left open due to the heat generated by the paraffin process. He trots up and down the aisles where the candles are poured in rows, checks everything out, and leaves through the back door. Lisa has seen the apparition at least six or seven times during the last year. Do you remember me mentioning Patty, Jacki's sister? Patty, whose office is closest to the production area near Lisa, has also seen the red wolf on a number of occasions. Two witnesses, one animal spirit, and a lot of questions... Why would the apparition of a wolf, or as the staff calls him Wolfie, visit a candle factory? And why does he only appear at the back door? Does he appear for a particular person, namely Lisa, during factory hours? Or does he simply retrace his steps from centuries ago, long before the area became industrialized? Hundreds of years ago, wolves ran rampant in this particular area, though the red wolf species is not common in Michigan. In nearby eastern Canada, however, a subspecies of grays, referred to as the Algonquin wolf, is a close relative of the red wolf.

Historical information on the area indicates a wolf habitat was located on the site now occupied by the factory. Although the area's settlers began building homesteads just after the War of 1812, farmers had begun establishing farms, "... just east of the railroad tracks," according to the book, *History of Oakland County*. Documents show that the area, including the site on which Coventry Creations now stands, was a problem for farmers in the form of wolves. The farmers in the area often spoke of the wolves that were, "...a constant menace to their farm animals."

The Investigation

After a brief tour of the building, the investigative team spread out and chose the areas they wanted to investigate. Keith, the director, set up his stationary camera, with audio, in the rear of the building, so that anyone–or *anything*–entering or exiting through the rear door would be caught on film. We chose one office, centrally located, in which to place a stationary recording device. The group set off in teams of two, with some flex time to work independently. Within the first fifteen minutes, two investigators began experiencing problems with their recording devices. One investigator, who charged her video camera prior to the investigation, found that after only a few moments of recording in the candle-pouring area, her battery had completely drained. When I attempted to make contact with a spirit in the lobby, within five minutes of asking questions, the tape recorder shut off on its own. Thinking the cassette tape was damaged, I gathered a new, sealed replacement tape to no avail, since the tape recorder refused to eject the current tape. I said aloud, in case the spirit was listening, that I really would like to replace the tape. Finally, the tape ejected and I replaced it with the fresh tape.

Out of the five investigators on the team, four had digital cameras; I had a standard 35 mm. There is constant debate over whether or not digital cameras or cameras producing standard photos should be used on investigations.

Many investigators enjoy the convenience of working with digital cameras. One of the benefits of digital cameras is that the photographer can see the shot immediately, then save or discard the shot at his or her discretion. This is especially convenient while shooting in an area where sudden activity increases during the investigation, for example, in a spot where temperatures fluctuate, a voice is heard, or the sensitive picks up energy, capturing an instant photo in the area. Advocates of standard 35 mm cameras argue that still photos can provide more detail than a digital shot, and that dust, particles, and other debris that cause false "orbs" are more prevalent with a digital camera, than with a standard 35 mm. Additionally, the photo negative works as a back up and can be compared with its corresponding photo when seeking out anomalies in various photographs. Some weigh the cost of digital cameras versus often lower-priced standard cameras, though others believe that the length of time and the cost involved in photo developing are burdensome. Regardless, our investigative group uses both, and having two different types of cameras provides us with a more thorough, well-rounded view—especially when both a digital and standard shot is taken of the same area at the same time—a visual form of checks and balances, so to speak. We also use two types of recording devices, both digital and analog, for the same basic reasons—to capture anything odd using two types of recording devices makes for a more thorough method of producing possible evidence.

The video camera captured an interesting image in one frame. After approximately two hours, a bright ball of light swoops down from the upper right of the frame to the lower left. The motion is accompanied by an animal sound, preceded by three of four seconds of the sound of water. Keith and Randy spent hours, afterward, narrowing the sound to that of a frog, though to me it sounded canine in nature. Either way, I can attest to the fact that neither a frog nor a dog was in the candle factory on a cold February night in Michigan.

After the investigation, I returned the following afternoon alone; I wanted to take general photos in the same areas we had photographed the evening before. It's wise for investigators to do this, if possible, so comparisons can be made between images of a specific area shot at daytime and at night. A large orb captured on a ceiling at night, for example, can be really intriguing. However it can be debunked by the same shot taken in the daytime, when that same area of the ceiling proves to be a water stain, not previously noticed in the dark.

It's interesting to note that the balls of light seen by the shipping manager is in the same room where I recorded a conversation prior to the investigation. I interviewed Lisa— she's the staff member who we believe attracts many spirits. During the conversation in the shipping and packaging area several days prior to the investigation, I asked Lisa to tell me about her attraction to animal spirits. The intention of the recording was not to capture electronic voice phenomenon, it was simply an interview process. However, when I went to transcribe my notes, I listened to the tape and found that, indeed, I captured a spirit voice.

During the interview, I asked Lisa to tell me about her experiences. She told me about some of the incidents relative to the factory. I then said, "Well, since we have the tape running, if there are any spirits who would like to make themselves known, feel free to speak." Then a low, masculine voice is heard, saying, "Don't talk." Lisa adds, "Yes, say something." Again, a spirit voice admonishes, "Don't talk." The spirit voice was not heard when Lisa and I held our conversation, it was only after I played the recording that we realized the two of us were not alone that day. Since the spirit advises another not to speak, we can pretty much gather that there were at least two spirits hanging around the table during the interview.

It would have been ideal to capture more images to match the voices and sounds heard at the factory, so that we could piece together who the spirit or spirits are that roam it. It also would have been great if Wolfie had made an appearance while we were there. But as investigators know all too well, sometimes we can't always capture it, even though we know activity exists in certain places. The variety of activity that occurs in the factory doesn't bother the staff in the least. To them, it's all part of the daily routine in a company that offers, 'candles, oils and spiritual goods.'

5

Grosse Pointe Character

"Every spirit makes its house, but as afterwards,
the house confines the spirit. You had better build well."

-- Elbert Hubbard
(who met his demise on the sunken ship, Lusitania, May 7, 1915)

Grosse Pointe Park

Whenever Katie and I get together, we usually wind up talking late into the night about our favorite subject—ghosts. Some people attract certain types of spirits. Katie has always attracted younger spirits. I recall spending summer vacations in northern Michigan exploring old cemeteries with Katie. One incident I recall vividly was a ghost of a young boy who would appear and reappear behind headstones wherever Katie walked—as if playing hide and seek with her. Perhaps Katie's ability to attract the younger spirits goes back to her childhood. She grew up in a home in Grosse Pointe Park and spent many nights communicating with a child on the second floor of the home.

Grosse Pointe has a special character all its own. It's actually comprised of five "points" including the Shores, Farms, City, Woods and Park. Katie's childhood home on Yorkshire Road is situated in Grosse Pointe Park.

To give you a visual of the area, Grosse Pointe in the late 1800s was the place where wealthy Detroiters had summer homes. These "cottages" were first built near Lake St. Clair and the region was the ideal place to enjoy the cool breezes the lake offered. Big names include D. M. Ferry, owner of the world's largest seed company; former U.S. Senator and Secretary of War, Russell Alger; and a handful of Great Lakes shipping magnates. After 1900, permanent homes began to replace the handful of cottages. Many of these permanent homes were designed for the families of automobile royalty like the Dodges and Fords.

I had visited the home on several occasions between 1988 until the home was sold approximately twelve

years later. The home is quite modest in comparison to the mini mansions in the neighborhood. I recall my first visit to the home in early autumn 1988. I was invited over for dinner, and had excused myself to use the first floor bathroom. I had grown up in an older home and knew how some ancient hardware on doors would often stick. In fact, I had seen these same types of locks on antique doors many times before—in the Penobscot Building downtown and in other older buildings. Funny knobs, skeleton keys, and the like that seem to twist one way or turn another. But this was very strange indeed. No matter what, I could not get out of this bathroom! I could hear everybody asking where I was and wondering what on earth I was doing. I actually looked through the keyhole and checked to see if the door was locked. Nope. Definitely unlocked. I pulled on the glass doorknob, thinking the door was just stubborn. Finally, after approximately ten minutes, a family member came to get me. He yanked on the doorknob several times and the door finally opened. Although this doesn't necessarily indicate a haunting, it bothered me enough to remember it in detail still to this day.

Regardless of the bathroom incident, I loved this house—it had beautiful hardwood floors and a winding staircase. When you stepped inside, there were these wonderful French doors that opened into a cozy living room complete with a fireplace and tons of books. The house just seemed like it begged for books, stories, and tall tales near the fireplace. The home had character all right. In fact, the *character* lived upstairs—only he wasn't among the living.

About a year or two after the bathroom incident, I received a call from Katie's mother. Would I be willing to spend a few days house sitting and taking care of their elderly cat while the family headed up north for the fall color tour? Hmmm...I could bring a buddy with me. I could hang out in that big old house in a great neighborhood. I was looking forward to it because they had cable TV and I didn't, and since I lived in a one-bedroom studio apartment at the time, cable TV was considered a luxury.

The first night was turning out to be quite un-restful. My buddy and I had settled into the living room and were all set for a long night of movies. The popcorn was popping in the microwave and all was merry. Then halfway into a Jim Carrey comedy we heard *IT*. Someone was traipsing around upstairs. I remember my heart racing. My buddy and I looked at each other, terrified. What the heck? This is one of the safest neighborhoods in the entire state. My buddy put his index finger to his lips, motioning me to be silent. Silent? I was ready to scream my bloody head off. I whispered, "*I'm calling the cops.*" He shook his head no. "It sounds like a kid walking around," he said. I had to admit he was right. The footsteps were light and quick...like a little kid doing a back-and-forth gallop through the upstairs bedrooms.

My buddy grabbed, of all things, a baseball bat that was used to prop open the basement door so the elderly cat could have access to the litter box at his whim. If I hadn't been so downright terrified I would have laughed out loud. He said, "You stay here, I'm going up there." I replied, "Over my dead body."

We stood against the wall near the staircase. Out of sight from whomever was prancing around upstairs, but within view of the upstairs hallway. And still the sound of the footsteps continued. I held the phone in my hand, with the police department already dialed so that all I had to do was to hit the "On" button. We stood there for what seemed an eternity, when my buddy slowly ascended the stairs. He tiptoed like some cartoon character with that aluminum baseball bat poised carefully behind his shoulder. I was frightened, yet the whole situation was strangely comical.

I imagined trying to explain the scene to the Grosse Pointe Park Police Department. The police in Grosse Pointe usually spend their Saturday nights busting up some party that got out of hand, wild parties held by teenagers who got sauced on single-malt scotch with Biff and Mindy while mummy and daddy were summering in the Hamptons. But how do I explain this one? "There's an intruder in the house. No, officer, I don't see him. He's *invisible*. No, officer, I haven't been drinking single-malt scotch."

We got to the top of the stairs and headed toward the first bedroom. My buddy did one of those action film kick-the-door moves. You know, where you jump to one side, weapon at the ready. We went through the entire upstairs. We checked under the beds. We checked the closets. There was no sign of a human being anywhere. We spent the next couple of nights with the baseball bat handy, but nothing strange happened after that. We told Katie about the incident and she did not seem the least bit surprised.

Katie told me that she had a pretty good idea who the invisible galloping culprit might have been. She explained to me that she suffered from insomnia as a child, due to a side effect from medication for an attention disorder. From her upstairs bedroom one night at age five, she heard a boy calling her name. She says that for the next three or four years in the middle of the night she would feel a strange sensation in what she referred to as "the coving area" — a small area between two doors in the hallway when both doors are slightly ajar. She says that every so often when the strange sensation was felt, a glowing light would appear near the coving area.

Katie mentions that although she was very young at the time, she was more curious than frightened. She also remembers snippets of conversations with the boy who would call her name. How he had to take medicine and how he also spent a lot of time alone. Katie describes her final encounter with the boy spirit as strange, yet enlightening. By this time, Katie was approaching her pre-teen stage and was already getting her hands on books about hauntings and paranormal experiences. She began to get comfortable with spirit activity and educated herself on different types of hauntings. Although she didn't know it then, this would be the final time she would ever communicate with him.

She explains, "I saw the familiar bright light near the coving area, only this time I heard his footsteps. It was the middle of the night. I knew it was the boy. I said aloud, 'Show yourself to me.' I heard an emphatic, 'NO!' He did not want to appear to me, for some reason.

Katie still remembers in detail what transpired next. When she insisted again that the boy make his appearance, the energy in the room began to change. At that moment, Katie watched the white light take on the shape of a small boy, *but only his arm and his hand materialized*! It was then that Katie realized that it wasn't that the boy didn't *want* to appear to her, it might have been because he *couldn't*.

We often look at the spirit world from the view of the living. Those on the other side have certain abilities, just as we do here. They may be adept (or not) at communication. They may be better at speaking than showing themselves. Some prefer to leave coins or other objects around the house. Others make noise. I truly believe that certain personality traits are carried over into our spirit form when we pass away.

The house has changed hands once or twice since Katie's family sold it several years ago. Katie has moved two or three times since then, but she will always hold a special place in her heart for her childhood home with its hardwood floors, inviting fireplace, wonderful books and, most of all, for its unique character.

Grosse Pointe Farms

In 1971, Linda and her soon-to-be husband, along with another couple, lived as renters in a home near Mack Avenue, a street that borders the city of Detroit and Grosse Pointe Farms. Situated in a quiet neighborhood, the three-story brick home is fairly modest in comparison to others in the well-to-do Grosse Pointe community. The home was large enough so that, over the years, it had several renters and, as it turns out, several visitors from the past.

The four of them invited a few people over one evening. A group of them stepped out to purchase soft drinks while the two couples that lived there remained in the house. Linda says that she and her fiancé were at one end of the living room and the other couple were at the other end when they heard what they thought was the group at the front door, returning from the store. The two women got up at the same time to head for the door. Linda states that the two of them were shocked to see a woman approaching them, wearing an antique, floor-length white gown. What was even more shocking than seeing a woman dressed in this strange costume coming by unannounced, was the fact that they could see *through* her. The woman looked at them, turned, headed toward a wall, and...vanished.

Within a year, another visitor came to the house. Linda's fiancé was lying on the sofa and felt the presence of someone standing nearby. When he looked over, he saw before him a stocky man dressed in an old-fashioned blue and white striped tank suit, which resembled a 1930s swimsuit, standing at the bottom of the stairs. The swimmer from the Depression era simply looked at him...*and then vanished*. Linda says that there was never anything threatening about the visits from these apparitions. The entire house seemed welcoming, though the basement often gave her the creeps.

Linda decided to find out more about the female apparition in white, and spoke with the woman who owned the home at the time. Thinking that the homeowner would be shocked to hear about the ghostly lady in white, Linda was surprised to find that the woman was nonchalant about the apparition. "Oh, that may have been my mother," the homeowner told Linda. She does that once in awhile. She likes to oversee things around here."

The homeowner, too, shared similar experiences with Linda that happened to her in the home. She told Linda that when she lived there with her three-year-old son, a frequent visitor would stop by. One afternoon the homeowner was in the basement doing laundry while the three-year-old rode his tricycle around the basement. The boy began speaking to someone. His mother asked, "Who are you talking to?" "Grandpa," replied the boy. "He's right here." His mother said, "Really? Can you tell me what grandpa looks like?" The boy began to describe, in detail, a man whom the mother knew quite well. Indeed, it was the boy's grandfather, whom the boy had NEVER met. "He told me his name," the boy said. The mother got chills in the basement that afternoon. Not only had the boy been born several years after the death of his grandfather, the toddler has never as much as seen a picture of the grandfather, let alone knew the man's name.

The strangest incident, however, took place a few years later in the home. A woman who was staying there was lying down in the living room and happened to look up at the ceiling. What she saw before her was a strange vision, much like a movie playing, of a man lying in a hospital bed. She thought it was odd, and the vision faded from the ceiling. But her thoughts instantly went back to the incident less than twenty-four hours later, when a stranger came knocking on her door. "Excuse me for being here on your doorstep unannounced," the stranger said, "but I felt the urge to come here. You see, I used to live here. And I just wanted to stop by and see the house one more time." Once inside the home, the women began to talk about the house. "One reason I felt the need to come by was because I was thinking about my late husband," said the stranger, as the two women walked toward the living room. "In fact," she added, "it has been one year ago yesterday that my husband passed away right here in this room." The woman began to wonder if perhaps the vision she had seen on the ceiling the night before was the stranger's husband. Or was it simply a coincidence? After all, the vision included a hospital bed, so maybe it was someone else she saw, like a patient at the nearby hospital or nursing home. She directed her thoughts back to the visitor.

The visitor continued, "My husband had terminal cancer, and we wanted him to spend his last days here at the house. So we ordered a hospital bed and set it up right here in the living room."

There have been different ghosts that appeared over the years to the people who have at one time or another stayed at the house on "M" Street. Whether the ghosts are related somehow or may just drift in and out at any given time may never be known. As mentioned, the house on "M" Street is situated on a quiet street. Things seem pretty quiet on the inside of the home as well—no poltergeists, no banging on the walls, and no moving objects. Just a few quiet visitors who every now and then make an appearance to those who decide to rent a room from the brick home on "M" Street in Grosse Pointe Farms.

The Cultural Center Comes to Life

"You know, all my life I have been waiting for an adventure. I thought it would never happen to me. I mean, adventures are for soldiers, or for bullfighters. Now, here I am. Paintings are moving and strange voices are calling for me at night, and all it cost me was five gallons of gas."

-- Lili Taylor, *as Nell Vance in 1999's "The Haunting"*

Founded in 1885 as the Detroit Museum of Art, the Detroit Institute of Arts, located on Farnsworth Avenue in Detroit's Cultural Center, has one of the most extensive collections of American art in the country. The museum's acquisitions also include a widely admired collection of European, Asian, and African art. Completely renovated in 2007, the DIA, as it is known among metro Detroiters, is home to such well-known works as van Gogh's self portrait, Diego Rivera's Detroit Industry frescoes, and the rare Korean piece, Head of Buddha. Additionally, the DIA houses works by such notorious artists as O'Keefe, Matisse, Tiffany, and Warhol.

The building itself is often referred to as an architectural masterpiece, as it was partially designed by Albert Kahn, a leading architect and close friend of Henry Ford. Take a leisurely stroll through its corridors and wings and, on your way out, admire a copy of Rodin's The Thinker, which stands guard outside its doors. But be sure to leave BEFORE the sun sets…because the quiet, aesthetic ambiance of daytime at the museum may not be so quiet after dark.

A guard at the museum has admitted that some strange goings-on have occurred deep in the night, especially surrounding two particular works. One, a tribal figure from a Kongo village, which was donated to the museum by Eleanor Clay Ford; the other, a painting entitled, "The Court of Death."

In the case surrounding the painting, "The Court of Death," which is hung in the American Gallery on the second level of the museum, loud crashing noises are heard at nightfall—long after the doors are locked. When security guards go to investigate what's causing the uproar, nothing is out of place. The loud crashing sound, the guard mentions, often resembles the sound of a work of art crashing to the floor below, though all works of art in the American Gallery are perfectly fine when the lights come on.

The painting, by Rembrandt Peale, was intended to describe how mortal man is called by death. The extraordinarily large painting was originally sent on tour in the 1820s and was touted as "a great moral painting." The concept for the painting was based on an award-winning poetical essay entitled, "Death," by a former Archbishop from England, Beilby Porteus.

A line from the famous essay states:

"But chiefly Thou, whom soft-eyed pity once led down from heaven to bleed for man, to teach him how to live. And, oh! Still harder lesson! How to die."

The essay won Porteus the Seatonian Prize in 1759. The Archbishop was an abolitionist known for his keen interest in the plight of West Indian slaves and who used his authority to challenge the church's position on slavery. He campaigned heavily against the slave trade and took part in many debates in the House of Lords.

Rembrandt Peale used the essay as his inspiration for The Court of Death, which depicts Death as a hooded figure in its center. The left side of the painting reflects images of humanity led astray by decadence, alcohol, suicide, and other frailties once known as sins, while the right side shows the image of humanity at war, trampling women and children. At death's feet lies the image of a young man in his prime, portraying the idea that death has no mercy for even the seemingly healthy and vibrant. An elderly man, arms outstretched toward the death figure in the center, is assisted in his final moments, by young Faith, who guides him gently to his final resting place.

The other paranormal event that has taken place on more than one occasion surrounds a statue simply known as the Nail Figure and which holds a prominent place in the African Gallery on the museum's first level. A security guard states that the figure was seen shuddering and vibrating, as if taking part in a tribal dance. What exactly is a "Nail Figure" and what type of powers does it hold? The nail figure, donated to the museum as part of a collection also donated by Eleanor Clay Ford, is a functional piece of art whose roots of origin stem from the Kongo people—villagers who dwell along the Atlantic coast of Zaire.

Also called Bakongo, the Kongo are a spiritual group who held tight to the belief of animism—objects that possess living souls. A nail figure, referred to nkisi nkonde by the Kongo people, is owned by the entire village. The figure was usually carved from a sacred tree and kept in a solemn place of honor. Nail figures were shaped like humans and were representative of land and sky spirits, as well as ancestral spirits. A nail figure was believed to carry powers to heal and was used in swearing solemn oaths. The nail figure played a central role in ritual where disputes were settled. Many couples that divorced would swear by the nail figure not to practice the dark arts against their former

Nail Figure, carved to capture the power of spirits, stands at the entrance of the African Art gallery in the Detroit Institute of Arts. The figure reportedly vibrates and dances after the museum is closed.

spouse, swearing to maintain civility. The nail figure's eyes, usually carved in large circles and often made of mirrors or the white clay found along the riverbed, would be able to ward off evil and would reflect the images of those who swear in solemn oath.

The faces of the oath makers, whether regarding land disputes or through a judicial situation, would be reflected in the mirrored eyes, holding them to their oath for eternity. The mouth and the eyes of the nail figure were often considered to be the channels between internal spirit powers and the external, physical world.

When a person of the Kongo village feared that a spirit had been offended, if two parties were in disagreement, or if an individual was experiencing undue hardship, a priest or diviner would be consulted. The priest or diviner would encourage the individuals to gather medicines, objects, and items of importance to add to a cloth bag referred to as a medicine packet. Once the bag was filled, it would be tied with raffia or wicker. The priest would then take the bound packet and place it in the belly or in the head of the nail figure. The belly of the nail figure was its central point of power, and when the medicine bag was inserted, the opening of the belly was sealed with a large cowrie shell or a mirror. Most nail figures were depicted with a beard and a grass skirt usually made of raffia.

The contents of the packet would sometimes include earth taken from graves of ancestors and white clay from the riverbed (the color white in Africa is associated with ancestors and the spirit world). Shells, feathers, animal fur, or mirrors would adorn the medicine bag. The term, "nail figure," is actually derived from the manner in which the participants of the ritual would seal their promise. Those who swore an oath would drive a nail or piece of steel through the figure, whereby the medicine bag would be pierced, activating its powerful contents and strengthening its energy. In Africa, metal is considered to be a prestigious commodity, adding honor and esteem to the spirits. The act of driving or hammering the nail through the nail figure would serve as a ritualistic and formal promise of good will or a seal of treaty, similar to Westerners signing a legal contract.

So does the nail figure really dance long after the last art lover has gone home for the night? One security guard swears that the figure takes on a life of its own. And that the crashing noises heard near the Court of Death painting in the American Gallery usually occur late at night. But, still, I had to get the opinion of another

security guard. After all, the DIA would not allow me to do a ghost hunt at the museum for security reasons, which is perfectly understandable. I spoke with a security guard and questioned him about the nail figure. His response was, "Oh, I'm not supposed to talk about that."

I interviewed another security guard on a recent trip to the museum. When asked about the Court of Death painting with its crashing noises, he stated that he personally has not heard any of the crashing sounds. His security post was usually in the African Gallery, which is where I was when I spoke with him. When I asked about the activity surrounding the nail figure and whether or not there have been any late-night tribal dances, he simply smiled quietly, his eyes locked in secrecy. He never did give me a straight answer. He didn't have to. He simply remained standing, keeping watch, a few feet away from the fascinating functional art known as the nail figure.

7

Animal Spirits

"For most of us, in this lifetime, or any other,
the most difficult moments of our lives
stem from the loss of a family member.
Let me tell you, without a shadow of a doubt,
our pets will be waiting for us on the Other Side."
-- Sylvia Browne, *Spirit of Animals*

have heard many heartfelt stories from people who have experienced mystical, spiritual, and ghostly encounters with their pets. People often say that some animal lovers have such a connection with their pets that the bond cannot be broken.

Ted Andrews, author of *Animal-Speak*, believes that animals, whether in physical form or in spiritual manifestation, appear to us for specific reasons. "The images of the animals and the expressions of nature help us to transcend our normal, waking consciousness so that we can more easily attune to ethereal realms and beings. The first step begins with realizing that all vision and imagery, originating in nature or the inner mind, has validity on some level."

Sugar

In the case involving J. D. and Ellen, a couple of cat owners, the companionship of one of their furry felines continues to this day...even *after* death. Ellen tells me that for years visits from past pets have occurred in her home. But recent incidents involving the

Sugar, a beloved pet, returns from the afterlife to enjoy snacks from his cat food bowl. His snoring can sometimes be heard by his former owners.

spirit of a cat who recently passed away confirmed her suspicions and she has no doubt that a loving companion can return now and then for a nap, a snack, or a bit of play time. For the past few years, J. D. and Ellen have had the pleasure of being the "parents" to two cats, a male, Sugar, and a female, Puff. Puff and Sugar were together for years. Sugar was the type of cat that loved to purr loudly, and eat loudly, as well. He also had a distinct snore.

Puff, the female, has always been perceptive to things around her.

"I have observed her for years, wondering what she is seeing," says Ellen. "She would just stare toward the wall, eyes as BIG as saucers."

One early morning, Ellen was enjoying her morning coffee, accompanied by Puff, perched comfortably on the back of the sofa. Ellen states that the early morning silence, except for Sugar snoring nearby, was broken by the sound of the pitter-patter of small paws walking across the kitchen floor. "Puff was on the alert and I could see that she was watching whoever it was. I got up and went to the kitchen, hoping for a glimpse. I could *hear* the sounds of an animal walking around the kitchen, but there was nothing there."

One of the most trying times in the lives of pet owners is the realization that our animals are ill or aged and facing the end of their lives here on earth. The thought of never seeing our companions again is often overwhelming. Do we have a spiritual connection with our pets? Ellen seems to think so. She recalls the difficulties in the last days of the life of her beloved Sugar, who became ill due to a diabetic condition. When he took a turn for the worse, she and J. D. took him to the vet. Sugar ended up in overnight treatment at an animal hospital. Ellen recalls what happened while she was at home and her cat spent his last evening on earth in the animal hospital.

"I was sitting with my coffee and crying my eyes out. There was no light on and my eyes were adjusted to the darkness. Only the light of the moon lit the room. I looked toward the doorway and saw a small mist come into the room. In just a couple of moments, it vanished. I believe that I saw his spirit leaving. The white mist rounded the corner and I knew that Sugar had not survived." Ellen's suspicions were confirmed the following morning, when she learned that indeed, her sweet companion had crossed over the previous night.

Within a few short days of the cat's passing, J. D. and Ellen began experiencing phenomena that had them both wondering if Sugar had returned to his comfort zones. "J. D. and I had settled down for the night and felt what seemed like a cat walking around on the bed. Sugar was a fairly large cat and we felt his weight pulling the covers down." Ellen also states that Sugar's distinct snore was heard recently. "I awoke in the night and began to hear that familiar snoring sound that Sugar would make. I didn't dare raise my head and look in that direction, I knew who was snoring." Soon, the sounds would be accompanied by something even stranger. On several occasions, both Ellen and J. D. heard the noise of a cat chewing on hard, crunchy food from the cat food bowl, with no cat anywhere in sight.

J. D. and Ellen believe that Puff, Sugar's companion, may be experiencing some ghostly interaction by Sugar, as well. Ellen says, "Once in a while, Puff will get all wound up, eyes wild, and will take off running at top speed. Just like when she and Sugar used to chase each other. Sometimes I see her looking around, as if Sugar is coming up right behind her. She'll jump to one side and take off running. Puff acts as if Sugar is right there with her."

Whether it's a quick afternoon chase with an earthly companion, settling down on the bed for a nap, or an occasional snack from the cat food bowl, it seems as if Sugar may be coming back for an earthly visit. Except for the misty apparition on the night Sugar crossed over, J. D. and Ellen have not seen Sugar in spirit form. The ghostly cat activity is proof enough for the two of them that Sugar comes back for visits. And that's OK with J. D. and Ellen who, as of this writing, are still experiencing ghostly cat phenomena without any valid explanation.

Jenny's story

This next story involves another cat, only this time the cat was very real and very much alive. A friend relayed a story to me involving a cat that had me scratching my head, for the mere fact that it is unknown who or what was doing the haunting. We know for certain the cat was real, but we don't know how it performed an action usually reserved for the two-legged species. Perhaps this kitty had a little help from a friend.

Ding Dong!

Jenny is the type of person who couldn't say no to stray animals. She especially loved cats and was prone to feeding stray cats and whatever or whoever else wandered over to her home. She found herself alone one evening and was enjoying some well-deserved solitude. It was a Friday evening, and Jenny was looking forward to languishing around the house. She had dozed off and on for several hours, when she thought she heard the doorbell ring in her sleep. She realized it wasn't a dream when, again, the doorbell rang. "What the heck... it's 5 o'clock in the morning!" Jenny thought that maybe her brother was stopping by...but this early? Anybody who comes calling at such an early hour is bound to bring bad news.

Jenny, half-asleep, quickly opened the door to find no one there. "Hmm...must've been a couple of pranksters," she thought. Looking side to side, she saw no movement, no one running away from the house. Then, as she was about to shut the door she saw *her*...a pretty little cat sitting perfectly still on the welcome mat. Jenny figured the cat was probably hungry, and would want a little snack before she went on her way. "Wait a minute...if the cat is alone, then WHO rang the doorbell?" Feeling a bit spooked, Jenny fed the stray and sent her on her way, figuring the cat probably belonged to somebody in the neighborhood.

That afternoon, the cat incident all but forgotten, Jenny puttered around the house going about her usual Saturday afternoon routine. She was in the middle of having a conversation with a friend when she was interrupted by the doorbell. She wasn't expecting anybody. Excusing herself, Jenny went to answer the door. When Jenny opened the door, she laughed in spite of herself. There sat the same cat in broad daylight, looking up at her, with *no* human being in sight. Once again, Jenny fed the cat and sent her on her way. Later that day, she tried to find out if anyone in the neighborhood was missing a cat and mentioned the doorbell incidents to a neighbor who got a real chuckle out of the story—until the neighbor became an eyewitness to the strange kitty who came calling, again, the following day.

Jenny was on the phone with the same neighbor with whom she discussed the strange encounter when, as if on cue, the doorbell rang. "OK, she told the neighbor, I am not answering that door. Look out your window and tell me what you see." The neighbor, who lived directly across from Jenny's house, looked out the window. Jenny's doorbell rang again, while the neighbor simultaneously looked through the window.

"You're not going to believe this," the neighbor told her. "I can hear your doorbell ringing through the phone, but there is no one at your door—except a pretty little cat sitting on your welcome mat."

Jenny convinced the neighbor that the kitty obviously wanted a home, though Jenny couldn't take her. The neighbor agreed to take the cat. Since that time the cat has happily embraced her new owner. As for Jenny, she still could not determine who or what was ringing the doorbell, trying to get her attention. Sometimes, the answers are too obvious to see. Perhaps the ghost was a lady who thought that Jenny could relate to a ringing doorbell and a cat for two simple reasons. Jenny is more than just a cat lover who sees to it that no cat goes without a good home and a good meal. And perhaps if there was a ghost trying to get Jenny's attention, the ghost chose the doorbell as a means of communicating the best way possible in a way that Jenny could relate to. You see, Jenny makes her living as an Avon lady.

An age-old question is still left to ponder. Do animals have souls, or are they simply faced with oblivion upon death? Many cultures have maintained the belief that animals are reunited with us on the other side. Despite the number of religions that

steadfastly insist that animals have no part in the divine scheme, Western civilization is slowly beginning to change its view on the concept of animals having the ability to cross over into the afterlife and, in many cases, give us signs that their spirits are alive and well.

No Pets Allowed

The small, two-bedroom apartment in southwest Detroit was perfect for Nellie and her roommate. It was in a fairly safe neighborhood, it was in close proximity to the nearby college where she attended school and, best of all, the rent was affordable. The only downfall was that the landlady did not allow pets. Nellie loved animals, especially dogs, but her mother was afraid of dogs and Nellie grew up without one. When Nellie reached age twenty and searched for a place of her own, she looked forward to renting a home or an apartment that would allow animals. Her mother convinced her to take the two-bedroom apartment offered in southwest Detroit and forget about getting a dog. "Dogs are trouble," Nellie's mother said. "You need to take them for walks, they need shots, and it's just one more mouth to feed."

Nellie resigned herself to the fact that she would put off her wish until the one-year lease was up before searching for a place where she could finally have a dog. But unbeknown to Nellie, she would soon get her dog—only this one would never need to go for walks, eat, or would require the services of a veterinarian.

"The first time I saw *it* I was so caught off guard that I dropped some dishes," Nellie said. "My roommate and I were in the dining room and had just finished eating dinner. I picked up the two dinner plates and a couple of cups and carried them into the kitchen. As I reached up to switch on the kitchen light, this little white ghostly creature came out of the kitchen and ran past me."

Nellie states that it was the size and shape of a little dog. When her roommate heard the crash, she asked Nellie what was going on. Nellie asked her roommate, "Did you see that? That thing...like a tiny white dog?" But her roommate had no idea what Nellie was talking about. She described the strange apparition to her roommate. "It was a furry-looking misty thing! You didn't see it? It scampered through the kitchen and came at me."

The strange incident was forgotten, until Nellie brought a friend over. The friend was a student who went to school with Nellie. It was Friday night and the two women had no money to go out, so they studied for exams, watched TV, and hung out in the apartment. It was getting late and Nellie invited her friend to spend the night. The young woman slept on the pullout sofa in the living room. Nellie says that just before sunrise, she heard her friend gathering up her things, run to her car, and drive off. She was puzzled, but figured maybe her friend had plans. She called her friend a few hours later and her friend began sobbing, "You've got SOMETHING in your place, Nell...*an animal ghost or something*. I was so scared I just had to get out of there. I was asleep and kept hearing this whimpering really close to me. Like a crying dog." Nellie told her friend that the noise was probably a stray outdoors. But the friend insisted that the noise was coming from somewhere in the living room. Her friend never stepped foot in the apartment again.

By this time, Nellie was getting concerned. She needed to talk to someone. Was the place haunted by a dog? Nellie had seen something; her friend had heard ghostly whimpers and, even if Nell's roommate had not experienced anything strange, there was definitely something going on. But how do you tell people there is a ghost in the apartment, let alone that the ghost is an animal? Nell figured she would ask the neighbor across the hall about the strange ghost. The woman across the hall had been living at the complex for years and was known to be a real busybody. "She knew everything about everybody," Nell said. When she ran into the neighbor in the hallway a couple of months later, she began a conversation with her by asking her if she believed in ghosts. "The woman told me in no uncertain terms that there is no such thing, and I decided not to pursue the conversation."

Shortly before her lease expired, Nell found new living arrangements. She packed up a few things and headed toward the car. The busybody across the hall spotted Nell and asked her if she needed a hand with the boxes. "I'm sorry to see you go," the neighbor told her. Nell explained that the house she would be renting had a lot more room—besides, she could finally get the dog she had been wanting.

"That's the problem with this apartment complex," the neighbor told her. "No pets. But that didn't stop the elderly woman who lived in your place before you moved in," she told Nell. "The woman died in the living room...on the sofa. Nobody wanted to tell you that, thinking you'd probably not want to rent the place."

Nell shuddered, thinking how she spent the last year in an apartment whose last tenant had lain dead in the living room. The neighbor continued, "By the time the apartment manager got to her, it looked like she'd been gone for quite a while. Apparently, she kept a little dog in the apartment, too. She probably didn't have the dog very long, or I would've known about it. But nobody suspected anything. That dog never barked. Never even made a whimper. Or I would've heard it. And I KNOW everybody's business."

"A little dog?" asked Nell.

"Yeah. That's why the landlady was so strict with you about the 'no pets' policy. It was a little white dog," the woman told her. "Poor thing. The dog had practically starved to death by the time the apartment manager had gotten there. I think they eventually had her put down or they took her to the shelter or something. I'm not sure if she survived. It's probably just as well, since the old woman had passed on."

Nell nodded in reply. She was sad when she realized what took place in the apartment, but was looking forward to moving on. She thanked the neighbor for her help and finished packing up the car. In a couple more days, she would be at her new place. Then she'd start looking for a dog—a *real* dog that could go for walks and scamper through the kitchen. Nellie says that a few weeks after she moved into the rental home, she stopped at the shelter to choose a dog and was given an application to fill out as part of the adoption process. Nellie says the first question on the application was, 'Have you had past experiences with pets?' She hesitated a moment or two before checking the box marked no, though she was quite certain that indeed, she had.

8

Time Travelers' Fashion Show

"Ghosts are a metaphor for memory and remembrance, and metaphorically connect our world to the world we cannot know about."
-- Leslie What, *Science Fiction Writer*

"We thought we were so cool back then," states Barb, who describes herself as an aging disco queen. During the late 1970s, Barb discovered a great nightclub off Harper Avenue in Detroit, where she learned the Hustle and joked about getting "Boogie Fever" on the weekends. Just a few short years later, Barb was still dancing the night away. It was the mid-1980s, the top forty dance hits and the fashions had changed, and Barb was working her way through college. She was an energetic waitress whose time was split between studying business during the week, working in a popular restaurant after classes, and then clubbing 'til 2 a.m. on the weekends. Her group of party friends included John, a close male friend who

Barb still describes as the best dance partner she ever had. When they weren't dancing to Madonna tunes or shopping for the latest fashions at the mall, Barb and John enjoyed watching scary movies or having in-depth discussions about the afterlife. Arm-in-arm, the two often took long walks on cool October nights through some of Detroit's reportedly haunted neighborhoods.

John sometimes talked about his interest in astrology, UFOs, and the possibility of life on other planets. He mentioned strange dreams that would turn out to be premonitions. Barb often told John about how she could point out all the houses, block after block, that she felt were haunted. John had never mentioned that the house he lived in was haunted, so it was quite a surprise for Barb to encounter something strange that night in the house back in 1986. But haunted it was, and nearly twenty-five years later, Barb still thinks about the night when "the ladies" came for a visit.

John still lived under his parents' roof on the notorious street, 8 Mile Road, which was later made famous by Detroit rapper Eminem. John enjoyed studying art, theater, and literature at Wayne State University. Barb lived in her parents' home, just two miles from John's house. Both in their early twenties and unencumbered, the two had a type of restless energy that often found them taking spur-of-the-moment day trips. With barely a thought about packing, the two of them would hop into the car and get away to the sand dunes on Lake Huron, the Irish Hills in the western part of the state, or spend the day in one of the pristine national parks in nearby Ontario, Canada.

So it was no surprise on a Saturday evening—May 24, 1986 to be exact—that another spur-of-the-moment getaway was about to unfold. During another evening spent under the pulsating lights at the local nightclub, John asked Barb to take a trip.

"Tomorrow is Hands Across America," he told Barb. "You know, we were talking about participating in that." The two had talked about the much-publicized event a few days prior. As part of USA for Africa, the gathering was organized to draw attention to hunger and homelessness. The event called for several million people to join hands that formed a human chain from Battery Park in New York to a pier in Long Beach, California. John had gotten information about a caravan in Michigan that would be heading out early the next morning, to join hands with a group in Toledo.

Barb recalls that the two had devised a plan of action. "We left the nightclub and stopped by my house to pick up a change of clothes for me, then the two of us crashed out on the sofa at John's house. John's mom was an artist and John told me that both his mom and his dad were out of town at an art gallery that was showcasing his mother's paintings. So we had the house to ourselves that night."

The two stopped at Barb's parents' house, where Barb grabbed her pajamas, toothbrush, a pair of white athletic shoes, and her matching navy and white jogging suit. She quickly threw everything into an overnight bag. Still wearing her "favorite '80s dance outfit," she and John headed to John's house. They made popcorn and watched MTV before settling down for the night. Barb vividly recalls the details of that evening, because what happened in the middle of the night still leaves her perplexed—and a bit resentful that John refused to believe her. Barb remembers specific details about preparing for the next day's trip to Ohio, especially how carefully she laid out her clothes.

"Now don't laugh," Barb told me. "But I'm going to describe what I had worn that night—my favorite dance outfit, complete with big, chunky silver-tone earrings and lots of big bangles on my wrists. The entire ensemble consisted of a long-sleeved shirt with a rainbow motif across the front of it, and a pair of what we called 'parachute pants.' They were form-fitting at the waist, then they sort of ballooned out, and then tapered at the ankle. There were little silver zippers at the ankle. I could open and close the zippers, depending on the type of shoes I wore, or if I just wanted to change the look. I also wore my absolute favorite shoes. They were short-heeled Mary Janes with ankle straps—basically they were tap shoes without the taps and they fit me like a glove. They were perfect for dancing all night in. But seriously, those balloon-looking parachute pants are what I remember the most. I must have looked like Mork from Ork!"

After arriving at John's house, Barb put on her pajamas and set up her weekend bag on a counter in the kitchen. John had set the alarm clock on the living room table, and set it to go off at 6:30 a.m. They would get up quickly, get dressed, stop for coffee on the road, and head to the assigned meeting place, a few miles away, before joining the caravan heading toward Toledo. Barb distinctly remembers setting everything up carefully, so that there would be no delays the next morning. She had written down the directions and a map to the assigned meeting place, the name of the person in charge, and the meeting time, and placed the information on the kitchen counter. She remembers that the kitchen at John's house had a short diner-type counter, a breakfast nook, with three or four wooden stools at it.

Barb set out her neatly folded jogging outfit and placed it on the counter next to the notes and the map. She took her "favorite dancing outfit" and her dance shoes that she had worn to the club earlier that evening and neatly placed them into the overnight bag. She zipped up the bag, and placed it on one of the kitchen stools. Directly under the stool, her white athletic shoes stood side-by-side, ready for her. "This way," thought Barb, whose busy schedule often called for quick changes, "I'll be sure to jump into my outfit, grab my bag, and be ready for the trip out to Ohio in the morning."

Finally the two dozed off—Barb slept on one end of the sectional sofa, while her buddy John snored away on the opposite end. What happened next is described by Barb as, "One of the strangest things that ever happened to me. I'm not sure if it was a time warp or what, but I truly believe that people from another era paid a visit to John's house."

It was still dark in the living room and the first light of dawn barely crept through the windows, when Barb was awakened by the sound of voices coming from the kitchen. It sounded like women chatting and giggling.

"I must say, I have never seen anything quite like this," a woman had whispered.

"Fancy these shoes!" said another. "I am going to wear them."

Fits of giggles accompanied the woman's comment.

Oh no...I think somebody broke into the house, Barb thought. *How many people were in the kitchen... three?...four?*

By now, Barb was wide awake. The sounds of people milling about the kitchen frightened her to the point that she considered hiding in the coat closet, just a few feet away. And why wasn't John hearing any of this? Still, the whispered voices continued.

"How do I look?" asked one woman.

"Oh stop," another said, in a fit of giggles, "You look frightful...I cannot bear it!"

More laughter followed.

Were these women trying on my clothes? Barb heard what sounded like her bangle bracelets hitting the kitchen counter, and the words the women used made it even more confusing. *Was it a theater group or something? I cannot bear it? Who talks like that?*

The sound of her personal items being ransacked was the last straw. Barb thought that maybe John's mother had come home. But there were at least two or three women's voices talking. She remembered that John had two sisters, one of whom she had met on several occasions. *But why were they talking like that...like Quaker women or something? And why were they going through her personal items?*

She recalls the strange light emanating from the kitchen. "It wasn't like regular electric lighting. It was bright, but the light seemed to bob in and out like candlelight," Barb told me. She remembers hearing more snippets of conversation about her clothing.

"Is she a gentleman?" asked one of the women, again followed by fits of giggles. "Then why does she wear trousers?"

"*Boy, these women are rude,*" Barb thought.

By this time the voices of the women were getting louder. "*John,*" Barb whispered, "*John...wake up. I think we're getting robbed.*" John snored even louder. She tried kicking him awake, but he was too far away, curled up at the corner of the sectional sofa.

"*What is going on here?*" she thought.

Barb states that out of sheer concern for her sanity—and the utter fear of seeing the intruders face to face—she slid down under the blanket and remained there for what seemed like an eternity. The chattering in the kitchen began to soften...until it was instantly silenced by the alarm clock going off.

John awoke and shut off the alarm. Immediately, Barb told him about the women in the kitchen. "I think your mom came home. And your sisters were here," she told him. She explained how they spoke like they were in a Jane Austen novel or something, using old-fashioned words. John, still half-asleep convinced Barb that she had a strange dream. He reminded her that his mother was out of town. And his sisters both lived on the other side of the state and would have no reason to come over in the middle of the night. "You were dreaming," he told her.

"At that point, I believed him. That was it. It was just a dream," Barb told me. She said that John got off of the couch and headed straight for the bathroom, while she approached the kitchen. There was no point in convincing herself otherwise. But she changed her mind when she stepped into the kitchen. Because what she saw convinced her that it was no dream.

"I remember that I was so shocked when I walked into the kitchen, that I lost my balance, and grabbed the wall to steady myself." Barb says that the neatly folded navy and white jogging suit was no longer on the counter, but was lying in a heap on the floor in the corner of the kitchen. Her white athletic shoes were askew, lying face down under the kitchen table, as if they had been kicked off and left there. The overnight bag was unzipped, its contents strewn across the counter in disarray. She hollered for John to come see for himself. John merely shrugged it off, and suggested that maybe Barb was sleepwalking and made the mess herself. "Hurry," he told her, "we're going to be late."

The two of them spent the day in Toledo, joining hands with those other seven million or so people, linking them together in Hands Across America that rainy day in May

89

of 1986. Barb remembers how a chairperson at the event talked about how bizarre it seemed to connect with those on the other side of the country, and how even though there were people hundreds of miles away, through the chain, we are really all right next to each other. Barb says her thoughts immediately centered on the strange event that unfolded the evening before, and that the statement was altruistic. After all, hadn't she been "right next to" other strangers who were miles away...only the chain was simply a thin line that connected those of the real world with time travelers from a bygone era.

Barb never spoke about the time travelers' visit to John again, and it wasn't too long after that when their friendship began to wane. John eventually moved down south. His parents sold the house in 1988. Barb found an apartment in the suburbs and a steady job in a quiet business office. "And I definitely got rid of my favorite dance outfit," she chuckles. "After all, fashion is constantly changing."

On rare occasions, Barb finds herself in the old neighborhood. The nightclub where she and John would dance the night away has long since been torn down and replaced by condominiums. She can't help but drive past the house once owned by John's parents. If it's late at night, Barb makes it a point to slow down long enough to see if there is any candlelight coming from the kitchen, and wonders if the ladies ever returned for an encore presentation of their fashion show.

Hauntings
at Greenfield Village

"The more enlightened our houses are,
the more their walls ooze ghosts."
-- Italo Calvino, *The Literature Machine*

The early "physical ghosts" of Ford Motor Company are long gone. Ford Motor Company's original plant on Mack Avenue in Detroit was destroyed by fire decades ago. The former headquarters on Schaefer Road in Dearborn was leveled in 1998, though the newer property is still retained as part of the Ford Motor Company. And the complex that once built fifteen million Model T's in Highland Park is an abandoned eyesore, with its overgrown weeds and broken windows. But the general public can relive the past at Greenfield Village, the brainchild of Henry Ford; it encompasses original or reconstructed buildings and homes once occupied by people of the day including the Wright Brothers, Noah Webster, Thomas Edison, and Robert Frost.

Henry Ford held long-standing friendships with such notorious inventors and entrepreneurs as Thomas Edison and Harvey Firestone, which fueled his ambition in gathering the minds and talents of like-minded individuals to share ideas, progresses, and possibilities of the future.

Unlike corporate executives and business owners during the heyday of the industrialization of America, Ford's desire to educate the public in the ways of transportation, inventions, patents, and industrial progress was equaled by his desire to seek retreat and find solace in working farms, cottages, and green fields—without the fortress-like structures of big-city corporate life. The culminations of these two widely different arenas, along with Ford's foresight to ensure the legacies of the past were preserved for future generations, resulted in Greenfield Village.

"The moment you step into Greenfield Village," touts the Visitor Guide, "you'll find yourself slipping into another era." I couldn't agree more—especially after hearing about some of the incidents involving apparitions and strange phenomena that seem to bridge the gap between now and yesteryear. Although many of the workers I spoke with deny any form of ghostly inhabitants along the Village's ninety-acre site, there were a few workers and volunteers who told me that the visitors themselves have revealed some interesting experiences. All of the stories are first-hand accounts—some were told by the volunteers and employees who, understandably, value their dedication to the Village and wanted to remain anonymous. Other stories were told to me by a couple of long-time visitors.

The Noah Webster House

Melissa recalls a visit to the Village with her husband and young son in 2001, and how lingering behind, alone in the Noah Webster house, brought back a memory of the same experience twenty-three years prior:

"I asked my husband to take my son, who was getting restless, out of the Noah Webster house and to wait outside. It was one of my favorite exhibits, and I didn't want to be disturbed by my child's unruly behavior. There were only a few people milling about, looking at the upstairs bedrooms, and I found myself alone on the first floor. I was looking intently at Noah Webster's earliest version of the dictionary, and thinking about how amazing it is that language and vocabulary have

A visitor in the 1970s felt a presence at this display of the original 1828 dictionary. When she returned to visit twenty years later, so did the presence.

evolved over the years. The dictionary, the wooden desk in Webster's private study, and other items in the Noah Webster house have always held a fascination for me."

Melissa then explains how a sudden presence behind her triggered a memory of an elementary school field trip years ago, to the Village, and she was in the same place.

"The other visitors had left. It became extremely quiet, and I was alone. I saw what appeared at first as a shadow approaching from behind me. There was a sense of somebody standing in very close proximity behind me, so close, in fact, that I felt this person breathing behind me. I heard no footsteps. Unless you are wearing socks or no shoes at all, it is extremely unlikely that you could walk around this structure, with its wooden floors, and not be heard. I know it sounds strange, but it wasn't fear that I felt—it was more like I was sharing the fascination of the exhibit with an invisible friend. At that moment, I had a flashback of the same exhibit, in the same place, with my elementary school. I was always interested in English and my school friend, Rhonda, despised English class. She hated spelling, her reading comprehension was poor, and I was forever helping her get through the basic rules of English. Anyway, Rhonda was standing next to me at the Webster home and I remember her saying, "This is boring." I responded with a wisecrack and kept looking at the 1828 dictionary. I remember her standing close to me, sort of behind me, watching me while I chatted to her for maybe a minute or two. When I got no response, I turned to look at her and there was nobody there."

A volunteer at the Webster house wanted to remain anonymous, to protect her position; however she corroborated the stories about the house and said that she often gets asked about eerie feelings on the premises.

"Just last week," the volunteer told me, "we had a problem with the lights flickering off and on again. Also, we have had people mention that they hear the sound of someone walking around in the bedroom of Rebecca and Noah's daughter, when there is no one in that room."

The Daggett Farm

The sounds of footsteps are not only heard at the Webster house, but they are also heard at an old working farm called the Daggett Farm. Samuel Daggett built the timber flank house in 1754 in Coventry, Connecticut (now Andover). He and his wife, Anna, along with their children, Isaiah, Asenath, and Tabitha, grew corn, wheat, cider, and tobacco. Sheep, pigs,

Daggett Farm is where two workers saw the figure of a man wearing period clothing. The figure was not in regulated Greenfield Village uniform.

and chickens were raised there too. The Daggett women were adept at spinning yarn, candle making, and soap making.

An employee who formerly worked at the Daggett Farm told me that she and another employee had arrived to begin their shift one early summer day. The two were alone on the first floor, and the employee states, "We heard the sound of heavy footsteps walking around the top floor. This was definitely the sound of someone wearing heavy boots. We knew for a fact there was no one else in the building at the time." Even after they checked to make sure no one else was there, the footsteps continued a few more moments until it was time to open up for the visitors to arrive.

Later, in autumn of that same year, the two employees again found themselves joined by an uninvited guest. The two were outdoors near the front of the farm and heard someone approaching. "We heard the sound of someone walking through the leaves, from a distance. When we turned to see who it was, we saw a man dressed in period clothing. He seemed to fit right in, though his clothing did not match the usual attire worn by any of the employees at the Village. He paid no attention to us, turned back around, and vanished."

A visitor contacted me about her recent experience at Greenfield Village. The visitor told me that she had stopped by several buildings throughout the day and took a total of 124 photos. She states that the moment she arrived at the Daggett Farm, she felt like the air was very heavy and that she was being watched. When she downloaded her photos, they all came out beautifully—except for the photos taken at the Daggett Farm. Every single one of them came out smeared.

While this does not necessarily indicate a haunting, many people say that cameras and other recording devices often malfunction or become unreliable when a ghostly presence does not want to be bothered.

Cotswold Cottage

In the infancy stage of Greenfield Village's development, Henry Ford searched for buildings that would illustrate the American way of life from the handicraft period to the industrial age. Often, his search took him across the country, and across the ocean, as well. Ford, along with his wife, Clara, enjoyed frequent visits to the British Isles, which increased their appreciation of fine art, architecture, horticulture, and craftsmanship. The two were especially smitten by the Cotswold cottages. The Fords felt that a Cotswold cottage would be a great addition to the Village, so that visitors could see the way in which many of our forefathers lived before migrating to America.

In the 1920s, H. F. Morton, an engineer in charge of the Ford plant in England was assigned to find the perfect cottage, and he found that cottage in Chedworth. As luck would have it, the cottage was for sale. Ford purchased the modest shepherd's cottage and had it torn down, packed, and shipped to its new home in Dearborn, Michigan. The property, completed in 1931, was then painstakingly reconstructed into exactly how it stood in the Cotswolds, including the original stone garden wall and the flowers that once bloomed nearby. A restaurant is now located inside the cottage and, on more than one occasion, a couple of the workers there have experienced ghostly activity.

A male presence is felt in the cottage, one worker tells me. "He doesn't bother the guests," she says, "but he's a bit ornery in the early hours of the day." He has been known to move items around that the employees have set up to start the day. "We sometimes have to tell him to knock it off, and usually the activity ceases…for a while."

When I asked another employee if she could add any other information about the purported ghostly activities at the cottage, she abruptly wished me a good day and ended the conversation. I took the hint and moved on. It's my guess though, that the spirits at Greenfield Village haven't.

10

Suicide on Haverhill

"It is required of every one," the ghost returned, "that the spirit within him should walk abroad among his fellow men, and travel far and wide; and, if that spirit goes not forth in life, it is condemned to do so after death."

-- Author Charles Dickens

There are as many views on suicide and eternal rest as there are religious doctrines that shape these views. One view, that of the older Hindu tradition (until the nineteenth century), was one of irony, to say the least. Called *sati*, it was a custom confined to certain castes and was borne of the belief that a woman had no value without a husband. Though not universally practiced, the custom meant the widow would commit suicide upon the funeral pyre of her husband, where she would remain to serve him in the afterlife as well as in future incarnations. The practice seems to contradict the view of the female considering the Hindus, for centuries, bowed before the goddess and held her female virtues in the highest esteem. This custom is no longer in force, except in some remote areas.

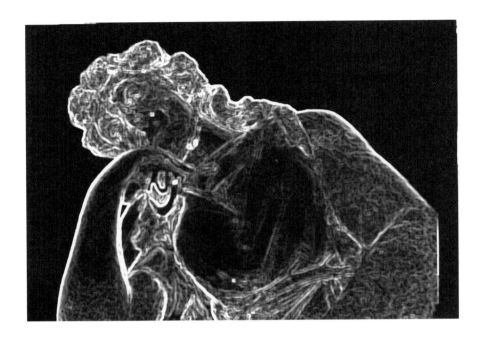

Judeo-Christian beliefs have held long-standing taboos against suicides. Though many Christian churches are beginning to show more compassion toward their views of handling the final repose of those who've taken their lives by their own hand, the Christian church believes, for the most part, that suicide is a mortal sin. These doctrines can, I believe, have major repercussions for those who commit suicide—long after death. Even if a person did not outwardly believe, during adulthood, that suicide is sinful, early upbringing may put the belief deep into the psyche. Upon death, deeply held beliefs may prevent the ability to cross over completely and face what is on the other side—especially the fear of remaining in a holding place, or what some refer to as purgatory. In Japanese cultures, it is perfectly acceptable to embrace suicide when conditions that call for loyalty and honor override the sense of defeat and perceived shame, as evidenced by the lives of the Samurai and the Kamikaze.

The Spiritualist viewpoint is one that leans toward the belief that there are many levels the soul may go through prior to attaining the highest level, which some call heaven. If a soul is unable or unwilling to let go, the spirit may be locked where the suicide occurred. Often, living beings claim to feel a heavy sensation in the air near the vicinity of a known suicide. This is most likely *residue* of human energy, which will, eventually, dissipate. I have also heard countless stories of those in **this** world who have done much spiritual work in assisting the souls of the lost. Of all the strange, unexplained, sad, joking, menacing, and bewildered ghosts I have encountered, there are none that I feel more drawn to, or more compassion for, than the suicides. The faithful side of me clings to the hope that most suicides eventually move to their highest place attainable through prayer and assistance from those left behind. The realist side of me has seen and heard enough to know that not all of them have the desire, the readiness, or the ability to do so. Such is the case of the suicide on Haverhill.

Vee was just a young teen when her family moved into the home on Haverhill Street in 1976. More than thirty years later, she can recall the oddities that occurred—and still occur—in the home, which is still occupied by her mother. "I get chills when I remember the times, during the summer, when us kids would be playing in or near the garage. There were several times when the heavy metal garage door would swing wide open, and then slam shut by itself. We got the impression that maybe someone was warning us to stay out of the garage."

Vee adds, "But the most memorable experience had to do with my father." She states that her father worked midnights at the local Ford plant and soon after the family moved into the house, her father was so terrified about an experience in the garage, he became sick to his stomach. He walked into the garage and got into his car. When he started the car, he felt something—or *someone*—in the car with him. There, looking straight at him, sat a woman in the passenger's seat...only the woman was not in solid form. He saw details of the apparition, who sat just inches from him, and distinctly recalls that she was attired in clothing from the late 1950s or early 1960s. He bolted out of the car and ran from the garage. Details about the apparition's outfit, including her plaid skirt, were forever embedded in his memory. Vee recalls that her dad was so shaken up about the incident, he refused to ever park in his own garage again, preferring to park in the street instead.

Shortly thereafter, Vee learned from a neighbor that a suicide had taken place in the garage several years prior to Vee's family moving into the home. Vee does not remember the details of the neighbor's account, but she does recall that the neighbor said the woman who committed suicide was around retirement age and may have been despondent over her husband's death. Shortly after his death, the woman drove her car into the garage, shut the garage door, and let the engine run, meeting her death by inhaling its toxic fumes. But did the woman completely cross over to meet her husband on the other side? After her father's strange visit by the ghostly woman in the car, and the kids being warned to stay out of the garage by the opening and closing of the garage door, Vee doesn't think so.

Vee's father was not the only family member to come face to face with the apparition, and the ghost itself began to show its presence in the house, as well as in the garage. And, after considering the type of activity that took place, Vee thinks the ghost may not have approved of smoking or of liquor consumption.

"We could always count on the ghost stopping by the house on the holidays, without fail," Vee says. "Every time the family gathered for the holidays, the family would have problems with the lights going on and off. There were occasions when the stove would not start, and then without any warning, it would start up again. Drinks would get knocked off the table. There were several times, especially at Thanksgiving and at Christmas, when a glass or two would slide off the table and crash to the floor."

The ghost also did not like smoking. Vee says, "One time, my brother was asleep on the sofa. He awoke to hear someone puttering about the dining room, wiping the table and clearing the area of an ashtray with cigarette butts in it. Thinking it was our mother, he sat up to say something to her. What he didn't realize is that no one else was there and it certainly wasn't our mother who was in the dining room."

Despite all of the unexplained activity, Vee's mother still remains in the house to this day. But Vee's mother does not put up with any ghostly shenanigans. Once, when the dishes in the china cabinet began rattling around by themselves, she soundly stated, "Leave my dishes alone!" The rattling stopped immediately.

Extended family members did not escape the activity doled out by the ghost either. Vee's brother-in-law was downstairs by himself one night, reading the bible. She says that her brother-in-law was interrupted by the feeling that someone was watching him. He glanced up and saw a woman staring silently at him. The figure, he claims, was attired in an old plaid skirt—the same woman who appeared in Vee's father's car three decades earlier.

Vee also states that the ghost made its presence known to Vee's sister when she was alone in the house. Her sister had put her baby in the crib and her toddler down for a nap. She went downstairs to do the laundry, shutting the door behind her. While in the midst of washing the clothes, she heard the familiar sound of her baby's walker. The walker repeatedly rolled back and forth quickly around the main floor, as if someone up there was pushing it around. Her sister, concerned that the little ones had awakened from their naps, ran upstairs to find the baby walker in the middle of the room, and her children sound asleep.

The reverend at the family's church has blessed the house, in accordance with the family's request. However, the reverend was not told about the haunting—Vee says that the reverend was told only that the house needed a blessing, nothing more.

A member of the clergy may be helpful in some cases. However, if the man or woman performing the blessing, cleansing, or smudging, is either a skeptic or not altogether versed in the ways of spirit communication, the blessing may be only a temporary fix, especially in the case of a suicide. It would be ideal if the clergy treated the suicide with gentleness in the form of forgiveness—letting the spirit know that he or she is free of the binds of self-imposed shame, "mortal sin," and regret. A blessing, rather than an exorcism, may break through the haunt, bringing closure to the deceased hovering near its former residence and allowing the family to live in a peaceful environment.

Vee says that the reason the reverend was not told about the haunting is that, most likely, he would not have come to bless the home if the family told him it was haunted by the spirit of a woman who took her own life. She mentions that after the house was blessed, everything stayed peaceful for a time. But the activity—though not as intense—started up again a few months later, and still continues to this day.

11

Stories

from St. Clair Shores

"They say that shadows of deceased ghosts
Do haunt the houses and the graves about
Of such whose life's lamp went untimely out
Delighting still in their forsaken hosts."

-- *Joshua Taylor*

The Counselor

R everend Selena K. is a counselor, Reiki healer, and doula. In her presence, you are immediately drawn to her charm, which is blended with a serenity that puts you at ease. Selena does not reveal to many people her ability to communicate with the spirit world. Yet, she states, "I have actually been doing this since the age of 12."

She has performed marriage ceremonies, assisted at births as a doula, and has worked as a counselor. So when she participated in a ghost hunt with a local group a couple of years ago, little did she realize that her skills as a medium would also entail counseling the souls of the dearly departed, as well. The ghost-hunting group had been asked to investigate a home in the St. Clair Shores area, a ten-minute drive from Detroit.

The location was at Jefferson, near Nine Mile, in a home where the family was in the process of putting the house up for sale. The family that lived there had two sons, ages 12 and 14, one of whom had been pulled up by the hair and thrown from his bed onto the floor. Selena received little information about the house itself, except that it was built in the early 1920s, and that most of the activity centered on the boys in the family. Though, the boys' mother also felt strange sensations. She'd sometimes find, when walking toward the boys' bedroom, that an invisible shield, like a brick wall, was put up with the feeling of, "You had better not go into that room." The feeling was also experienced in the hallway and the pantry.

Upon entering the house, Selena was immediately drawn to two spots. One in particular was a small closet or pantry area that held old shelving units. She got visions of five steps and a staircase. Selena was right on target—the area was formerly a staircase that was now blocked off, with a room added around it. Selena put her hand against the wall and said she felt a force throw her hand back away from the wall. She then went over to the boys' room, where most of the poltergeist activity took place. Her back was to the closet in the bedroom and at one point she was sitting forward.

"The spirit of a man appeared before me," Selena says.

At the same time the spirit communicated with her, the members of the ghost hunting group captured unidentified sounds on their recording devices. Orbs were also picked up in the area, on film. Selena asked the male spirit a question and her head was instantly slammed back against the headrest of her chair, as if an unseen pair of hands yanked her back by the hair. In the early 1920s, Selena later found out, the former staircase, now blocked off, and its remainder used as shelving in the pantry, was the scene of a murder. The male ghost that appeared to Selena in the bedroom threw his wife down that flight of stairs, where she died at the scene. The couple had four children, who grew into adulthood.

While Selena was at the house, the spirits of the four children returned in the form of children, not the form in which they took upon their respective passing, in adulthood. Does this seem strange? Not the way Selena explains it. She states that the four spirits returned in the form of children because that is where their initial sensitizing event occurred. This was their childhood home. By the four spirits coming together in the home in which they grew up, the home in which their father threw their mother down the stairs, they could better assist Selena with putting together the events of the past…and get to find the eternal peace they may not have had when they lived there. The children led a very isolated existence inside the home, during that turbulent time after the passing of their mother. The spirits of the children told Selena that, within a year of their mother's death, the father had taken in a housekeeper.

However, unknown to those in the neighborhood, the housekeeper, a young, attractive black woman, was actually a gay, black male. Back in the 1920s, it would certainly have caused a scandal—a white man taking in a young black man, posing as a woman. The issue about the "scandalous lifestyle" of their father was not what the children were concerned about. In fact, their issues were more clandestine—and more heartbreaking. The children, in their isolation, were faced with a nightmare that they took to their graves. Their father's lover had molested all four of them. In today's world, there are safety nets available that assist children who are dealing with molestation. They are told to tell a teacher, an adult, anyone, and are (hopefully) removed from the environment.

Keep in mind this was the 1920s, and the children lived in an extremely isolated environment. Taboo would be an understatement. With the death of their mother, the appearance of their father's lover, and the continuous molestation throughout their childhood, the children were, indeed, troubled souls. The father, it was revealed, was extremely controlling. Selena states that when the spirits of the children communicated with her, there was so much anger coming into the room. Selena actually managed to counsel the four spirits in their reverted child states. Consider that the children grew up into adulthood, yet returned, in spirit form, as they were when they were children, in the very home where the dysfunctional activity occurred—where do you find the words to console the young spirits who seek to let go of their anger? Selena took on the challenge, and spent quite a bit of time with them. She assisted them in releasing their anger and guiding them to return, peacefully, back to the other side.

The Farmhouse

In a northern suburb of Detroit, just a quick drive from the Nine Mile exit off of I-94, lies a wonderful old farmhouse on the corner of a quiet two-lane street. The home is the oldest one in the well-maintained neighborhood that still retains a close-knit feel to it. It's the kind of neighborhood where banners advertise the annual Memorial Day parade and fireworks announce the arrival of the Fourth of July. The farmhouse is reminiscent of days gone by. It's so old, in fact, that even the name of the street is the same name as the family who built, and first owned, the original homestead. At first glance, the farmhouse, built in 1875, appears as if it stands in a time warp. Its structure seems oddly out of place in a neighborhood mixed with condos, stores, a modern house of worship, and nearby World War II-era bungalows. When Matt R. first bought the old farmhouse in 1990, he knew there would be plenty of work ahead of him. Most of the wooden framework had to be refinished, steps and stairs needed fixing, and plasterwork had to be redone. Arches above windows that once held stained glass windows had been plastered over—those needed to be torn out and brought back to their original beauty. But the house seemed to call to him, and he knew he had to have it.

The black asphalt road that welcomed visitors in the 1970s and wrapped around the side of the home would, thankfully, be replaced twenty years later by Matt. He saw to it that the asphalt was taken out and replaced with landscaping and gardens that would artistically accent the brick structure to complement its original 1875 country ambiance. Matt called his home renovations "a labor of love." From brick replacement, to updating the electric work, to completely overhauling the kitchen, it's no wonder he called it that. The little touches throughout exemplified Matt's devotion to creating a haven, as he puts it; a respite from a demanding but fulfilling job, frequent business trips, and the need to relax in a cozy environment. So cozy, that a few *lingering* guests, or should I say, ghosts, decided to stay a century or two.

Matt begun planning the renovations from the very beginning. He had accumulated fabulous artwork by a local artist and had an eye for design, color, organization, and interior decorating, the whole nine yards. With no children and a busy career, he anticipated spending nights relaxing by the fireplace, especially after doing reconstruction on the weekends. What he did not include in his blueprints was providing accommodations for those in the spirit world. We laughed, the two of us, about the ghosts who hang around and cause a mess or two, but then don't clean up after

109

themselves—like the ghost who hovers in the kitchen...but I'll get to that in a moment.

I stopped by on a rainy spring afternoon, to hear Matt's stories. One of the first things he told me was that he often feels that the spirits who take up space there should probably pitch in a bit more around the house. "Hey, I figure if they're going to hang around here, the least they could do is to give me a hand now and then," he says.

The home has a real draw to it. In fact, while looking for the address while driving down the street, I saw the home and before I checked the address, the voice inside me said, "Go no farther. This is it." What I would soon discover is that before the day was over and my interview with Matt was coming to an end, I would experience a hint of a ghost myself—up in the attic—at that wonderful old farmhouse.

When I first walked into the home and stepped onto the long, wooden porch, I instantly felt at ease. "Any spirits that would possibly hover over this place are surely not evil," I said to myself. I felt that there was at least one young spirit there. In fact, I was *convinced* that there was a child spirit there—I pegged the spirit as a young male, around age 13 or so. I was wrong, I soon discovered. The spirit that hangs out here was younger, and was female.

Matt welcomed me in and began to tell me what he knew about the history of the home. He bought the home in 1990, and has spent, to his estimation, $130,000 on remodeling and repairs. When the major renovations took place, the spirit activity increased, which is usually the case. "But the activity is also random—and it usually happens when I am alone in the house and everything is quiet," Matt tells me.

He showed me copies of photos taken years ago by the former owners—grown women who spent their years growing up in the home. Matt keeps in touch with one of the former owners, an elderly woman who is still perplexed about an unexplained incident that happened to her when

Farmhouse in St. Clair Shores. Its current owner, on three occasions, has heard noises in the kitchen and has found the kitchen chairs rearranged.

she was just a child. But first, Matt wanted to tell me about the kitchen. It was completely torn out and refurbished and since then, on at least three occasions, Matt had the unique experience of dealing with a ghost or two who felt that the kitchen layout was not to their liking, and decided to let him know about it at 3 a.m. He tells me that he was upstairs, alone in his room, when he heard the sound of a kitchen chair being dragged across the floor. He then heard the other kitchen chairs moving until he realized that all of them were being moved around. When he ran downstairs, he expected to find a burglar, stranger, his partner Dave... anybody. What he found were the chairs, repositioned. The bizarre incident has replayed itself on two other occasions, again only when it's extremely quiet, usually at 3 a.m., and when Matt is the only one home.

He also tells me about the "cold breezes." He states that sometimes, with no natural explanation, he feels like he's being watched and the feeling is then accompanied by a major temperature drop. So cold, in fact, that it feels like a cloud that circles him and actually passes *through* him. But he admits that none of the supernatural feelings or occurrences he has experienced have been overtly negative. It's almost like child's play. One of the most prominent "cold breeze" incidents happened a couple of years ago. He was on the staircase that leads to the upper floor, and was having a conversation with his partner Dave. Oddly enough, the two were discussing whether or not there was a possibility that ghosts may be staying with them. It was in the middle of winter, and the heat was on. The doors and windows were shut tight. There were no vents or windows near where Matt stood at the time. Yet right in the middle of the conversation about ghosts, along the staircase, the temperature dropped several degrees and the cold breeze not only passed by the staircase, Matt claims it felt as if it moved right *through* him.

Most of the strange feelings he gets usually are on or near the staircase. As mentioned, the previous owners have kept in touch with Matt and Dave, and one of the daughters of the family who lived there for many years before selling the home to Matt, recalls her days growing up in the home. She related an incident to Matt involving, once again, the staircase.

The former owner told him that she found an antique doll on the stairs when she was a young girl. The doll simply appeared from seemingly nowhere. The girl, alone on the stairs, began to play with the doll. For the next several minutes, she enjoyed looking at her and playing make-believe. She turned her back for a moment and when she swung around to reach for the doll, it vanished. The girl trotted off to find her mother and asked her, "Have you seen the doll? The one that was on the stairs?" The young girl described the doll to her mother. Her mother told her, "You don't have a doll like that. I do not know what you are talking about." The girl insisted that just moments before there was an old doll on the staircase and, while playing with her, the doll simply vanished. The girl began to look throughout the old farmhouse and, disappointed, gave up hope and returned to the staircase. That's when she looked up and realized there was one place left that she had not searched—the attic.

Alone, the girl began to look through the attic and when she reached an old, forgotten storage area near the back, she saw a large wooden barrel with a lid on it. The young girl pulled the lid off of the barrel and discovered the container was filled with toys and miscellaneous items. She quickly pulled out toy after toy, item after item until she reached the bottom. There, stuffed at the bottom of the barrel, was the doll. The elderly woman told Matt that she recalls that between the time the doll disappeared and the time she found it, no siblings were around and there was no way possible for anyone to have taken the doll without her knowing

Staircase in the farmhouse where its former owner, as a child, experienced an antique doll materialize, only for it to disappear and then reappear in the attic.

about it—after all, the doll had been right next to her on the stairs. One moment it was lying next to her; the next, it dematerialized, and then a short time later had materialized in the attic, stuffed at the bottom of a barrel.

The doll incident can be described as an example of an **asport**, a physical object from a known location that disappears and is found in a remote location without a valid, scientific explanation, though some may refer to it as a form of telekinesis. That is, some believe that the catalyst that makes the object disappear and reappear is actually a person, or agent. This is also commonly noted among situations involving a pubescent child. Whether the materialization and dematerialization is a direct result of spirit activity or subconsciously directed by the child, the result is still phenomenal.

The elderly woman also relayed a story to Matt about her brother. She stated that many years ago, not long after the doll incident, one of her brothers was in the attic and passed by a large mirror. He saw movement out of the corner of his eye. The boy glanced into the mirror and saw the image of a young girl in a little gown from another era. Her full image appeared, and she was holding a blanket. She simply looked at him...*and then slowly disappeared*.

My tour of the home and the interview with Matt was winding down, as he told me about one more incident, this time involving a relative. In 2003, he hired his cousin, an electrician, to do some electrical work, which involved going into the basement and working in a crawl space directly underneath the kitchen. As Matt was out of town at the time, his cousin let himself in, and the unsuspecting electrician soon began setting up his equipment. His cousin later told him that he removed a wall panel that leads to the crawl space so that he could reposition a line below the house. He got to the end of the crawl space–approximately twenty-five feet–and the lights turned off on him. Making his way through pitch-blackness, he came back and checked the lights. Everything should have been working properly. The lights in the basement turned on again. The electrician shrugged indifferently, went back to the crawl space, and began his odyssey again. And again, when he reached twenty-five feet, everything went dark. Beginning to get a little uneasy, he returned through the darkness, and checked the lines in the house again to ensure everything was working properly. Within seconds, the lights came back on. A third attempt was made. When he made it through the crawl space, he was, once again, left in the dark. At his wit's end, the electrician scrambled back through the dark, packed up his tools, and hasn't returned since.

As Matt finished his story about the electrician, we left the basement and headed back to the main floor. There was one last area we hadn't looked at yet—the attic. Matt wanted to show me the area where the doll had mysteriously reappeared in the attic...just a few feet from where the little girl appeared in the mirror. When we got to the attic, Matt began speaking and we made our way to the back storage room. When he reached up to pull the chain on the light switch, there was a brief burst of light in the room, and then the light turned itself off. Matt said, "Hold on a minute," and returned a moment later with a new light bulb. He began speaking about the doll and showed me where the large mirror once hung so many years ago. He inserted the new light bulb and the light came on... only to shut itself off again in a matter of seconds, when he spoke about the image in the mirror again. We laughed about it and neither one of us needed to state the obvious. I figured that was my sign that maybe somebody up there wanted to be left alone. Perhaps she was telling me that I might have overstayed my welcome. We made our way back to the main floor and I wrapped up my interview with Matt.

He reiterates that he does not feel anything menacing about the spirit activity, but he admits that he sometimes "gets the creeps" when he's alone in the house. The hair on the back of his neck stands up when he hears the kitchen chairs moving and he knows there is no one in the kitchen...a bit of a shiver runs down his spine when a cold breeze envelops him on the staircase...and he knows there is no natural explanation when the lights go off by themselves. But Matt is realistic. He knows that any major renovations that take place in the farmhouse will kick things up a bit. He understands that the ghosts that hang around his place do not plan on leaving anytime soon. So there is nothing left to do but find humor in the situation. With a wry smile, and a firm nod of his head, he states that when the activity starts, he calls aloud to nobody in particular, "If you're NOT paying rent, then get out." Matt tells me, as he escorts me out to the front porch, "It works every time. The activity stops immediately."

Thus ended my visit to the wonderful old farmhouse in the northern suburbs of Detroit. As I headed to my car, I stood for a moment to enjoy the gentle rain as it nourished the old-fashioned garden that complemented so well the brick farmhouse built nearly a century and a half ago. The overcast sky was the perfect setting to step back and take a photo or two of the farmhouse that seems to stand in a time warp. I took one last look before quickening my pace as the rain began to pound more heavily. The early evening thunder only added to the eerie feeling of an oncoming electric storm that usually hits in the springtime, when the warm, moist air combines with the cool breezes from Lake St. Clair. It was the kind of storm that brings with it goose bumps on the arms and the urge to seek comfort in a safe environment. I made it back to my car, just as the thunder clapped a few feet from the farmhouse. As I pulled away, I took one last look in my rearview mirror. My gaze went to the attic window, hoping to catch a glimpse of a little girl from another century, holding a blanket. She did not make an appearance. I could have sworn though that, just for a split second, the light in the attic dimmed, then brightened, only to burn itself out again.

12

Motor City Madness

"The lawn is pressed by unseen feet and ghosts return
Gently at twilight, gently go at dawn
The sad intangible who grieve and yearn"
— *T. S. Eliot*

From ghosts to an evil-looking dwarf to a statue that has animated, legends and lore abound in the Motor City. Some of the following stories have been retold or handed down by early settlers, while others have been described in detail by eyewitnesses. Enjoy the following stories about some of the more popular legends of Detroit, which take place along the area of the Detroit River. Some date back more than three hundred years.

Belle Isle

It was in early spring in 2008 that Sheila Anderson decided to take Claire, her teenage daughter, out to spend the day at Belle Isle. Claire was out of school for spring break, and the two spent the afternoon driving around the downtown area. Claire was beginning to show an interest in architecture and design, and Sheila wanted to show her some of the island's late nineteenth century structures. The two rolled down the windows and enjoyed the short drive along the General MacArthur Bridge that connects the city to this historic island. Native Americans once called it Wah-na-be-zee, or Swan Island, and was eventually changed to Hog Island, before it got its current name, Belle Isle.

Once described as the "jewel of Detroit," the city acquired the six hundred-acre island from Americans who purchased it from the British. Its original ownership was traced to French settlers before it was overtaken by the British during the French and Indian Wars. The island was renamed in the late 1800s, and its renovation into a city park was inspired by the tree-lined boulevards of Paris. But this jewel in the city, where Victorian-era athletes once engaged in rowing contests in the summer, and a young Henry Ford, in his derby hat, was known to enjoy ice-skating along the sleek winter ponds, was not without its problems. As the twenty-first century unfolded, Mafia henchmen were reported to dispose of a body or two on late-night trips across the bridge, and the area was also the scene of major disturbances during the 1967 riots.

Sheila and Claire wound their way down Strand Drive on the island and parked the car. Together they walked the small footbridge over Lake Tacoma, discussing the history of the island.

Sheila and Claire then made their way toward the statue of Major General Alpheus Starky Williams, former Michigan commander and war hero of both the Mexican War and the Civil War. The statue, Sheila told me, has a strange presence about it. Here is Sheila's eyewitness account about what happened next:

Statue of Colonel General Alpheus Starkey Williams.Some say the statue appears to turn its head, and some see its eyes move. *Courtesy of Sheila Anderson*.

"The two of us pulled off the road at Inselruhe and parked the car. I wanted to take some photos of the statue. The statue is mounted pretty high and stands at a crossway. But there were very few cars around, so it was easy to approach. I read the inscription, which mentioned Williams' legacy. He is mounted on a horse and is holding a map. Anyhow, I said out loud that I couldn't get a good shot of his face and the horse at the same time. I walked around to the other side and I could swear his head swiveled, ever so slightly."

Sheila mentions that she probably figured she imagined it and that, since she had been looking up at the sun, perhaps her eyes were out of focus, until Claire spoke up.

"Mom," Claire said, "his face *turned* to look at you!"

Sheila said that her skin got prickly, though she was standing in bright sunlight. Claire began to get antsy and giggly and said, "... that guy is creeping me out." Sheila quietly scolded Claire and told her to be respectful for the military man on horseback, while she snapped another photo of the statue. When she turned to face Claire, she saw her lurch forward slightly and then whirl around to look behind her. Puzzled, Sheila approached Claire and asked her what she was doing. Claire's high-energy demeanor suddenly changed.

"Somebody with a large hand grabbed me by the shoulder," Claire said. "Like someone was reprimanding me!"

Sheila tells me that she figured it might have been the Major General, telling Claire to "straighten up." Or it could have been a sign that the two were no longer welcome. With a whispered apology to the statue of the Major General, Sheila collected her wits and her teenage daughter, and headed for the car.

The two then drove around to the forest area along Tanglewood Drive. Reports over the years have stated a misty woman in white has been spotted moving through the woods. According to Marion Kuclo in her book, *Michigan Haunts and Hauntings*, the misty woman in white also transforms herself into a deer. This account of **shape-shifting** is based on the popular legend of an Ottawa chief who wanted to protect his beautiful daughter from suitors. So stunning was she that the overprotective chief sent her along the river in a covered canoe, which would take her to a beautiful island uninhabited by man. The daughter was free to roam the island, where she would spend her days among the deer, the otter, and the magnificent forests and lakes.

Sheila and Claire walked briefly through the forest area, where the birds chirped peacefully and the trees were beginning to show signs of renewal after a long winter. No sign of the white lady appeared, and that was okay with Sheila and her daughter. The strange statue experience was enough for one day, though they plan a return visit soon to the island.

Nain Rouge

Little Harbinger of Doom

His origin is unknown, but his presence is unmistakable. Early settlers of French origin dubbed him, Nain Rouge, or Red Dwarf, and he is said to appear just prior to doom or an uprising. It began as early as the 1700s, when Antoine de la Mothe Cadillac, the founder of Detroit, spotted a strange creature resembling a gnome, with animal characteristics. It has been described as having piercing eyes, rotten teeth, and a darkish red fur. Soon after spotting the hideous creature, Cadillac lost his fortune and his political standing.

In July of 1763, the British planned to take severe action to stop Chief Pontiac and his warriors from overtaking Fort Detroit. Except for Forts Pitt and Niagara, the Detroit fort was the only remaining fort still under British command. Captain James Dalyell, a young up-and-coming British officer was appointed to thwart the takeover. He was known for his leadership, his bravery in facing dangerous situations, and most of all for his hatred of the so-called "red man." What he did not know was that many of the French traders were spies and had witnessed Dalyell and his two hundred British soldiers arriving in the middle of the night, headed toward Fort Detroit along the Detroit River. Major Henry Gladwin opened the fort gates to allow the entrance for Dalyell and his entourage. They held a meeting inside the fort, where Gladwin begged Dalyell to be careful. After all, Dalyell was not familiar with the fort layout, Detroit's terrain, and the methods used by Pontiac.

Dalyell paid no heed and hastily put a plan together. He and his troops marched a mile and a half at night, out to Parents Creek, near the Native Americans' encampment. The notorious Red Dwarf was seen wandering the banks of the Detroit River and was said to have been stalking Dalyell just before dawn on that fateful day, July 30, 1763. But Dalyell feared nothing. Crossing the rickety bridge over Parents Creek, Dalyell led his men toward the encampment where, unbeknownst to the fearless British Captain, Pontiac and his entourage were already lying in wait. By the time Dalyell ordered his men to retreat, the damage had been done. The Parents Creek Bridge swayed unsteadily with the weight of the dead British soldiers. Later, survivors recall seeing the creek running red with blood in the early morning hours. The battle and the creek were then known as Bloody Run. Whether it was a sign of what was to come, the appearance of the Red Dwarf strikes an interesting theory. Perhaps red was the symbol of warning: the British, dressed in red, the creek running red with their blood, as they tried to annihilate the "red man" seems tied together somehow. Once again, the Red Dwarf had made his appearance prior to disaster.

Multiple people witnessed other appearances of the Red Dwarf in 1805—they saw the figure prior to the great fire of 1805, in which a majority of the city's wooden structures burned to the ground. And just seven years later, General William Hull, in the short-lived War of 1812, had spotted an eerie child-size creature in the fog along the banks of the Detroit River...prior to surrendering Detroit to the British.

An attack on a woman took place in 1884, by a creature who resembled a baboon with horns. The victim stated that the creature had a devilish leer on its face. A similar attack was reported in 1964. Witnesses reported seeing the Red Dwarf roaming the area of 12th Street on a hot summer night in July of 1967. Within twenty-four hours, the city of Detroit made national headlines and then-U.S. President Lyndon

B. Johnson called out the National Guard as all-out chaos erupted in a hostile race riot known as the 1967 riots. By the end of the four-day riot, nearly five hundred injuries were reported, forty-three people were dead, more than 2,000 buildings had burned, and 7,200 arrests were made.

Nine years later, during one of the coldest winters on record, two utility workers reported seeing what they originally thought was a child climbing up a utility pole. In an attempt to reach the child to bring him to safety, the workers were shocked to see that it was actually a dwarf-like creature, which then jumped several feet to the ground from the top of the pole and scampered off. The following day, the city came to an abrupt halt with one of the worst ice storms in its history.

More recently, two gentlemen spotted a strange creature making crow-like noises. The last reported sighting of the Red Dwarf was made by two nightclub patrons out late one night in 1996. The two claimed that a small hunched-over man wearing what appeared to be a nasty fur coat was spotted making strange "cawing" noises, like that of a loud crow. The creature was seen fleeing a car burglary. Whether the Red Dwarf is a demon, a delusion, or direct premonition of disaster, no answers have been forthcoming and probably never will. For now, the Red Dwarf has not made his presence known in the last ten years or so. Let's hope, for the city of Detroit, it remains that way.

Scott Fountain

Final Revenge

Although Scott Fountain at Belle Isle is not necessarily haunted, we can pretty much guess that the man for whom the fountain was built probably turned over in his grave for at least fifteen years. That's how long it took between the time ol' James Scott passed away and his bequest for a fountain in his honor commenced. Perhaps though, this was the city's way of retaliating and having the last laugh on Scott, long after his passing. And why not? It was Scott himself who pulled a joke on the city, and this story is just one more strange misadventure in the madness of the Motor City.

When it was announced in 1914 that famous architect Gilbert Cass had won the design competition to build the James Scott statue and fountain near the foot of the Belle Isle Bridge in Detroit, the *New York Times* hailed the soon-to-be-built memorial as the most costly memorial of a person willed by himself.

Upon its completion, the gleaming white marble fountain was a sight to behold. The outer pool of the fountain is 112 feet in diameter with inlaid Pewabic Pottery tiles and its main, central column bursts water forty-feet high. Beautifully sculpted images of loggers, pioneers, and Native Americans surround its Vermont white-marble main base. And more than a hundred water spouts are designed with a myriad of lionesses, Greek-style drinking horns, water nymphs, dolphins, and more. Brass turtles pay tribute to Scott from below, spewing crystal clear water in a breath-taking architectural scene typical of the Romanesque style.

But the turbulence that occurred between Scott's passing and the completion of the statue makes for an interesting twist.

When James Scott, the only surviving offspring of a well-to-do real estate mogul, died in 1910, no surviving family members could be found. When his will was opened after his passing, imagine the delight to the city council members! He had bequeathed his entire fortune–a half-million dollars–to the city. New paved roads could be had, or perhaps an updated trolley system, or maybe improvements to the public schools.

It seems that James Scott had other ideas. The only way the city could use the money, his will stipulated, was to have a fountain built featuring a bronze statue made in his likeness on beautiful Belle Isle. Scott, it was discovered, detested most of Detroit and its citizens, rubbing elbows only with fellow gamblers. Although some say he tipped the newsboy well and tolerated children, others claim he despised the kids, often throwing rocks at those who dared to step on his lawn.

When word got out about Scott's final "in your face" joke about using the money for his likeness, citizens demanded that the city refuse to accept the money. Scott, they claimed, was a lazy loud-mouthed scalawag, who inherited the money from his well-to-do father, a hard-working real estate investor. Unlike his father, James Scott never worked a day in his life. The only memories the city had of Scott were his filthy stories, off-color jokes, profanity, and shady real estate deals. He once got revenge on a neighbor, who refused to sell him a parcel of land that he wanted to add to his property on Peterboro and Park Streets. Scott so despised the neighbor for not selling him the land that he spent $20,000 to build what appeared to be a fancy addition on the neighbor's side. Upon closer inspection, it was only a façade, attached to a shack with a high wall, whose ugly presence was solely to block the neighbor's view...and the chance of the neighbor from getting any sunlight from that side of the street.

Scott had an enemy list a mile long and no close friends, except for a few poker buddies. The scurrilous misanthrope remained a life-long bachelor and seemed to delight in frivolous lawsuits, scandal, and vindictiveness—using his money to take revenge on whomever he felt deserved it.

As the years progressed, meetings were held among Detroit politicians and dignitaries to decide the fate of the generous windfall. The prominent Detroit businessman, J. L. Hudson, was quoted as saying, "The fountain would be a monument to nastiness...Mr. Scott never did anything for Detroit in his lifetime." So intense were the feelings of those who reviled Scott that the memorial debate lasted nearly fifteen years. So much money was available, yet nobody wanted to spend it. In 1914, the city held a competition among designers and the feat (or as some considered, the task) was awarded to well-known architect Gilbert Cass. One Detroit clergyman suggested the size of the bronze likeness should be equivalent to the moral stature of the man, and suggested a two-and-a-half inch statue, "so as not to deter from the beauty of the fountain."

It seemed for a while that the joke was on Scott. However, even long-gone and buried, the shrewd Scott once again let his money talk, and got his revenge. Ironically, the initial dollar amount quickly gained in value and the city had no choice but to spend the money...soon. When the completion of the statue and fountain commenced, the entire worth of the bequest had gained in value to nearly one million dollars. It took another eleven years to complete the endeavor, and the entire lower end of Belle Isle had to be reconstructed to handle the process. Marble staircases were added and more details in the design were incorporated, until the last of the money was spent. The statue and fountain were finally dedicated May 30, 1925, with little fanfare. For fifteen years, the city gambled with the idea of not accepting the money. But like the vengeful spirit he was, the boorish gambler held the final winning hand. Many visitors have stopped for photo opportunities at Scott Fountain. For years, children who have most likely never heard of James Scott would scramble atop his statue, poke him in the eyes, and pose on his knee. Finally the city, citing safety issues, will no longer allow kids to climb the statue, even if it meant getting a bird's eye view of the fountain. A sign that reads, "Keep Off!" now rests sturdily upon the lap of the statue, which, I am most certain, would have suited James Scott just fine.

The Henry Clay

Spare These Stones

In July of 1832, a steamer, the *Henry Clay*, carried troops to fight in the Black Hawk War. Originally headed to Chicago, the steamer landed in Detroit to unload passengers afflicted with cholera. This set off a disastrous incident that changed the course of settlers and those who came to the city to seek work and build their homes. By the time the epidemic had completely swept through the city, with the additional second influx in 1834, thousands had perished. Many deaths went unreported, due to spotty record keeping. Within a few days, ninety-six citizens perished in just the local "parish" alone—at the vicinity nearest the ship docking. Hundreds more would follow the same demise.

This deadly disease is spread through contaminated food and water. Once infected the victims succumb within a few days, most within twenty-four hours. The death rate, at the time, was fifty percent. A group of German immigrants arrived, and shortly thereafter, many Irish immigrants. Locals warned the immigrants to leave. Bridges leading into the city from various waterways were torn down to prevent newcomers from entering the city and armed men were stationed outside the city to prevent ingress. Early documents recorded the description of the epidemic by stating that, "...people were thrown out of hotels. Mail carts were ordered to stop and all the passengers were questioned before entering neighboring towns."

The captain of the *Henry Clay's* accompanying ship, the *Thompson*, later described the scene that early July day in 1832, as the *Henry Clay* temporarily docked near the mouth of the Detroit River where it meets Lake St. Clair.

> "*The Henry Clay arrived at Detroit a few hours in advance of the Thompson, and while lying at the deck two deaths occurred on board from the cholera. This created such alarm that the authorities of the city prevailed upon the captain to leave the dock. On my arrival at Detroit, I found she lay at anchor near the foot of Hog Island [Belle Isle], some two miles above the city. Up to that time no signs of cholera had appeared on board my boat. After remaining a short time at the wharf, taking on board fuel, stores, etc., for the trip we got under way and went alongside the Henry Clay.*"
>
> "*The next day, the Clay arrived at the St. Clair River. The disease had become so violent and alarming on board of her that nothing like discipline could be observed. Everything in the way of subordination ceased. As soon as she came to the clock, each man sprang on shore, hoping to escape from a scene so terrifying and appalling; some fled to the fields, some to the woods, while others lay down in the streets and under the covert of the river banks, where most of them died, unwept and alone.*"

The city was thrown into a situation of utter madness. Silas Farmer, who recorded much of the early history of Detroit, wrote, "Businesses were suspended to such an extent that grass grew up in the middle of the principal streets and at night tar barrels were used to disinfect the air and lit up the night sky. The tolling of the church bells for the dead was so continuous that it oppressed the living and they begged for relief from the fearsome sound."

A nearby plot of land at St. Anne's parish, plotted for cemetery use fifteen years earlier, filled up quickly and became the final resting place for those who succumbed to the first outbreak. More bodies were buried two years later at the second cholera outbreak. Due to the need for more burial space, Woodlawn Cemetery was founded and later, Elmwood Cemetery. Then, in 1860, the area of the original cemetery was dug up to make room for new buildings and progress deemed necessary by the city. Workers were summoned to undertake the daunting task of removing the headstones and disinterring thousands of bodies long-since forgotten and buried deep in the original cemetery plot. The remains were moved to both cemeteries.

Among the bodies buried there was that of a gentleman named Nathaniel Hickok. A rudimentary slab of slate above a sunken grave outlined in cobblestone read, "In memory of Nathaniel Hickok, who died of Cholera. October 6, 1832." The tombstone also included the same words that occupy the tombstone of William Shakespeare, believed to have been written by Shakespeare himself:

Decrepit tombstones add an eerie feel to the city's oldest cemeteries. One legendary tombstone, similar to the ones shown here, came with a curse.

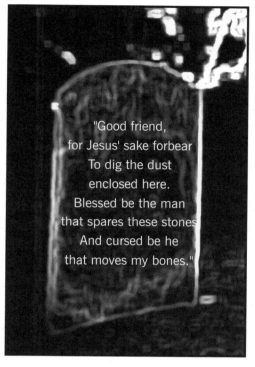

"Good friend,
for Jesus' sake forbear
To dig the dust
enclosed here.
Blessed be the man
that spares these stones
And cursed be he
that moves my bones."

Every worker who was assigned to the project had stopped to read the inscription before moving on to dig up the next grave. The foreman of the project demanded the workers to open the grave of Nathaniel Hickok, but the men refused to touch the cobblestones, the bones, or the headstone. For weeks, the work continued around the moss-covered slate slab warning of impending doom to those who dared move the bones below. When it reached the point of complete impasse, the workers took drastic measures.

Word around town was that a handy and hard-working gravedigger at Elmwood Cemetery was willing to go beyond his duty, but was reportedly addicted to stimulants. Some said he was illiterate, others claimed he was an immigrant who couldn't speak English. Regardless, an "extra reward" was promised to the willing gravedigger, who soon accomplished the task of disinterring the bones and its accompanying slate engraved with the curse.

The disinterred remains of Nathaniel Hickok rest peacefully at Elmwood Cemetery among beautiful landscaping, chirping birds, and lush, green meadows. The fate of the workman is unknown.

13

The 20-Minute Lesson on Hauntings

"I could well imagine that I might have lived in former centuries and there encountered questions I was not yet able to answer, that I had been born again because I had not yet fulfilled the task given to me."

-- *Carl Jung*

Growing up on Detroit's east side instilled within me an appreciation of old homes. Summertime meant the windows were wide open, and brought with it the sound of foghorns from the freighters along the Detroit River and Lake St. Clair. Crisp autumn days signaled the coming of Halloween. The wheel of the season turned and Michigan's ice storm knocked out the power lines to our old Victorian home, meaning the candles would be lit, casting eerie shadows on the walls.

My childhood and teen years in the late 1960s and early 1970s included tuning in to TV shows like "Dark Shadows" and "Twilight Zone"—or local programs such as "Sir Graves Ghastly and the Ghoul." I remember the simple thrill of eating Jiffy Pop and drinking Tang while watching Vincent Price movies on the black and white television (until 1972, when the family finally caught up with the rest of society and purchased a color television set). Perhaps I was destined to explore the darker side. Although I spent many years reading and learning about ghosts, and wandering into places where I would feel something strange, it wasn't until 2002 that I joined an official paranormal investigative group and finally got hands-on experience in the field.

My experiences as a paranormal investigator have been sometimes routine, partly exhausting, many times exhilarating, and left me empty-handed, but they're always plain, hard work. Devotion to the cause, endurance, and commitment to hours of analyzing data are paramount. Ghost hunting programs on TV make the hobby of paranormal investigating look exciting (which it is). However, what the audience at home does not see is what ends up on the cutting-room floor at the TV studios, most likely hours upon hours of filming that captures nothing out of the ordinary. In other words, for every investigation that may turn up possible "proof" of a haunting, there are a dozen more where the investigators come up empty handed. That's not to say that just because nothing showed up on film or tape means a place is not haunted. Most times, the odds are left to chance. But if you are serious about seeking out ghosts, be prepared to devote several hours to fieldwork, research, meetings, travel time, and analyzing data. Maybe you do not desire to become a paranormal investigator and simply want to be more aware of ghosts in your own home or place of business. Or maybe you are just interested in the subject matter. Whatever the case may be, here is some basic information about hauntings.

Why Do Ghosts Return?

This is one of the great mysteries of the universe. Studies in the paranormal realm are based on theories that cannot be completely and unequivocally measured from a scientific standpoint, so we are constantly going back to square one—the debate about whether or not ghosts exist. The idea of a spirit surviving after death to return to this world in a form that is visible but not comprised of material that can be analyzed is difficult to explain. There is not one parapsychologist, paranormal investigator, medium, technician, or spiritual advisor whose theories or opinions can provide proof of ghostly existence. In basic theory, nobody knows the truth. But those theories can be based on personal experiences, studies, data gathered from investigators, eyewitnesses (especially two or three who have experienced the same phenomena), historical information, and much more. Some return because they can't move forward, some return by choice, and some are simply stuck halfway through both worldly veils and don't know where they are going. To me, ghosts are very real; the problem lies in the fact that it is extremely difficult to verify their existence.

Throughout history, there have been reports of phenomena in various cultures. As is typical in the realm of parapsychology, there is much controversy as to the validity of ghostly visits. Quantum physics and its related studies of matter and energy is an exact science supported by theories, measurement, and conclusive evidence. Paranormal phenomena are subjective and its data and analyses are left too much interpretation. No scientific proof has surfaced to completely and unequivocally prove to—let alone convince—the general public, that ghosts and related subject matter exists. That being said, I believe that with the advancement of technology and the ever-increasing interest in parapsychology, it will not be long before a connection will be found to bring the two together.

Still, there will always be those who will never be convinced. Skeptics and non-believers actually help, rather than hinder, the advancement of understanding ghostly phenomena. Because their role is one of skepticism, they are extremely helpful in debunking, reasoning, and seeking plausible, proven reasons for hauntings. This contributes to the need for advancement of scientific research of paranormal investigations. So, moving beyond whether or not ghosts exist brings us to why anyone, after crossing over into the next realm, would return. The following offers suggestions and probable reasons why ghosts return:

> † To complete unfinished business.
> † To convey a message that was left unspoken.
> † For fear of facing judgment in the afterlife.
> † In retaliation.
> † Due to anger or sadness at having left too soon.
> † In response to a request from a loved one.
> † To console grieving family members or spouse.
> † To affirm to loved ones that they are o.k.
> † To convey approval/disapproval of decisions regarding marriage, property, career, children, heirlooms.

Where the Ghosts Are

† *Ghosts may remain on their former property*. Years ago, people cultivated their land. It was everything to them. They built their homes, often using hand tools. In essence, their blood, sweat, and tears were there. Their energy was deeply entrenched into their living space. Even as recently as a hundred years ago, women gave birth in their homes. Funerals were held in homes. The life and death cycle

135

generated in the home and on the homestead. And the former landowners or its residents held that connection, I believe, sometimes after death.

Nowadays, homes can be built in less than a month, people are "flipping" houses, getting rid of their homes so quickly and there are fewer emotional ties to the home or property. The energy is fleeting.

That doesn't mean the newer homes are not haunted, though. In my opinion, the older homes usually have a resident ghost while the newer homes are haunted by someone related to the family.

† *Ghosts may remain where a violent death occurred.* It is believed that violent deaths contribute to ghosts returning. This is especially evident in the many documented ghost sightings reported at Gettysburg, Pennsylvania. More than 600,000 deaths occurred during the Civil War, including nearly four hundred suicides. Add to this the fact that most of the soldiers in battle were young and those who died in combat succumbed to their demise in a slow and painful manner. By this I mean that hand-to-hand combat often results in maiming, lost of limbs, bleeding to death, and intense suffering, as opposed to death that is quick and, physically, less painful. Other "hot spots" include scenes of murders, fatal car accidents, and areas of natural disasters that claimed many lives at once.

† *Ghosts may remain where their death was self-inflicted.* It is my personal belief that, except for the loss of child or infant, no death is as unexplainable or more painful to deal with from the perspective of surviving family members and friends than death by suicide. For years, many personal attitudes and religious beliefs made the act of suicide even more painful for those who grieved the loss of a loved one. Some considered death by suicide a mortal sin, adding the

weight of shame and sadness to an already unbearable loss. Often, the body of the victim was not allowed burial on sacred grounds, leaving the family with little choice in where to bury their loved one.

The guilt family and friends experience *(i.e. "I could have prevented it," "How come I couldn't see the signs..." or other typical expressions)*, may add to the length of time of grief. This culmination of emotion can result in the soul of the deceased to be unable to move forward. There is no doubt that grief, anger, sadness, confusion, and other emotions hold us, here on earth, in a state of stagnant behavior. It is only when we move from that stage to acceptance that we move ahead. Wouldn't it also make sense that those who have crossed over experience that also? Other people theorize that suicide automatically places the soul in a place of limbo.

There have been many reports of people seeing apparitions repeating the last, final steps taken before their own suicide. I have always thought that perhaps some who have crossed over by their own hand may be stuck and try to instantly reverse their decision upon crossing over. Remember, time has no meaning on the other side and some may simply keep repeating the death process over and over for centuries, not knowing where to go or what to do.

† *Ghosts may remain if their lives were not honored or acknowledged.* Popular destinations for paranormal investigators include asylums, hospitals, orphanages, and other institutions due to the massive amount of paranormal activity reported on or near the properties there. Popular places in Michigan (many of which have been since torn down) include Eloise Insane Asylum, Jackson Prison, Traverse City State Hospital, and the Hillcrest Sanitarium. Eloise Insane Asylum, built in 1839 was at one time the largest asylum in the United States. The 902-acre site was closed

down in 1981. Prior to the type of mental healthcare we have available today, the care received by those who were pegged as insane was abysmal. These are the places where families, police departments, neighbors, strangers, or relatives often dropped off societal "rejects."

Those who were illiterate, born out of wedlock, homeless, physically or mentally handicapped, and those with every type of malady or disease from depression to alcoholism were subject to being locked up and out of the public eye, many of whom remained there until their demise. Death from experiments, disease, malnourishment, suicide, and abuse was common. Sadly, upon death, no family members were able to (or wanted to) claim the body, and mass graves can still be found around some of the properties. Numbers marked most graves while many more were not marked at all. It is believed that some who die without some type of honor or acknowledgement of passing are likely to return.

Signs of Hauntings

There are many signs that may indicate a haunting. Some signs that draw suspicion include:

† Unexplained shadows that dart, weave, or grow across walls

† Objects that seem to disappear for a day or two, only to reappear in another room or in a place where said object would not normally be found

† Lightbulbs that flicker or burn out faster than normal

† Sudden breezes, wind, or drafts that cannot be explained

† Extreme and sudden changes in temperature

† Crackling noises, heavy static, erratic radio frequency

† Footsteps, knockings, or rappings—especially knockings that seem to come from inside the walls

† Water faucets, electrical appliances, or battery-operated devices that turn on or off by themselves. Also, batteries that have been fully charged that drain instantly in particular rooms

† Scents that seem oddly out of place—tobacco or pipe smoke in smoke-free homes or buildings, fresh flowers in the middle of winter, floral perfumes in homes uninhabited by women, or masculine scents in homes uninhabited by men.

† Coins, feathers, small jewelry, or other items that appear in a prominent place or area where the items would be noticeable

† Uncanny coincidences or signs that cannot be ignored—especially seen in three's or over a three-day time period (this is usually related to familial or ancestral hauntings)

Attempting to Find the Source

You do not have to be psychic or even intuitive to find ghosts. Using common sense and deductive reasoning can help you draw conclusions that may pinpoint the type of spirit that haunts a given area. It is highly recommended that if you experience recurring hauntings, as opposed to sporadic ones, you should set aside a notebook (or start a document on your computer) to help you keep a record of the presumed paranormal activity.

† Jot down the following information: What type of activity occurred, in what room or area, any feelings associated with the activity, the date, time, weather, and any pertinent information about the time period, such as recent upheavals in the home (divorce, new baby, plans to move, redecorate, news from relatives, new marriage, etc.).

† Consider where the activity takes place and what type of activity it involves. For example if the spirit activity is close to the ground—say three or four feet, involves mischief, hiding small objects, or if giggling and singing are heard, the ghostly culprit is most likely a child.

Activity that seems heightened in the kitchen is usually related to a female spirit. Garages, dens, or activity surrounding tools usually involves a male spirit.

My theory is that if the paranormal activity occurs on holidays, birthdays, anniversaries (especially the anniversary of a death), usually it's an ancestor or family friend paying a visit. If it occurs during a renovation of a house, redesigning the garden, painting a room, moving in or out of a house, or making major changes to living arrangements, the spirit is usually related to the property or the house itself, though sometimes the spirit will favor one particular family member over the others. There are, of course, spirits who contradict this, since not all female spirits and male spirits haunt "traditional" male or female-related areas. Remember, these are general guidelines and each ghost is different. To further assist you in attempting to find the source, take a look at the types of ghosts you may run into.

Types of Ghosts

† *Messengers, Protectors, Spirit Guides.* This type of spirit is usually a spirit guide, guardian angel, a deceased ancestor, or someone connected to the viewer through bloodline, marriage, or other close tie. Ancestors, spirit guides, guardian angels, and similar "helpers" fall into this category. Most sightings of this nature occur at times of undue stress, in times of danger, before surgeries, or during special days recognized within a family, i.e., weddings, anniversaries, birthdays, and holidays.

† *Resident Ghosts or Residual Hauntings.* Paranormal investigators who are called upon to investigate haunted houses or other buildings are likely to be very familiar with this term. Some resident ghosts are also categorized as

earth bound spirits. The resident ghost may have lived in the house prior to its current occupants inhabiting the home, may have died on the property, or may have resided on or near the property before the home was built. This is one of the most common types of sightings, and I have experienced this type in my own home on a regular basis. The longer a person or family owns the property, the more likely the person's energy is rooted into that area, thereby increasing the likelihood of returning to its roots, so to speak. When it comes to haunted buildings, the haunting is usually by the business owner or an employee—especially those whose duties were held long term. Many people define themselves by what they do. Some feel so connected by their duties here on earth that even when they cross over, they find it difficult to leave their work behind.

Resident ghosts can be connected to anything from a famous landmark, to a commercial building, or even return to enjoy watching us mortals in our own homes—most likely the homes that once belonged to them. Although some resident ghosts have an affinity for a specific person in the home or building, the connection is usually to the physical place itself, rather than with the people who inhabit it. The resident ghost will often make his or her presence known during construction, renovation, or when a homeowner or renter moves in or out.

† *Lost Souls and Earthbound Spirits*. These are troubled souls, to put it mildly. The earth bound spirit is most likely—but not always—a resident ghost. The difference is that resident ghosts, in my opinion, are not necessarily *always* earth bound. I believe that some resident ghosts can come and go at will, whereas the earth bound spirit either cannot or will not find its way out. I have dealt with resident ghosts who, with the assistance of a medium, know full well that they are dead, have been to the other side and back,

and have no intention of leaving permanently. Some have unfinished business, and will not rest until they accomplish what needs to be done. Many factors may contribute to keeping a spirit earthbound. Popular theories include that the earth bound spirit or lost soul is tied to remaining family members, material possessions, or the refusal to accept their own death. Other earth bound spirits remain victims of their own fear, including facing judgment for the wrongdoing and evil they've committed on earth, or—for deceased victims of abuse—fear of meeting up with their tormentor on the other side.

† *Hostile Entities and Poltergeists*. These types are, categorically, the most physically active and violent type of ghosts. Typical poltergeist activity includes appliances turning on and off by themselves, knockings, repeated opening and closing of doors, the lifting, moving, or the throwing of knives, pens, or other projectiles, and unseen physical attacks to an occupant. The activity is usually aimed at one household member or property dweller in particular—and most documented cases overwhelming show that in the homes or buildings where poltergeist activity takes place, there is at least one family member, usually female, who is going through puberty or adolescence.

Further studies indicate that the increase in poltergeist activity often parallels the increased emotional upheaval of the pubescent or adolescent child. There is some controversy over the cause and the increased elevation of poltergeist activity. Researchers debate whether the poltergeist feeds on the energy and psychological changes produced by the child (or "agent"), or whether it's the agent who causes, through psychokinesis, the unseen forces with which the inanimate objects move of their own volition.

Anyone who has experienced a hostile or malevolent entity, especially those entities that appear as black shadows, knows that fear, that deep-seated terror, that encompasses us and shakes us to the core. So what is the answer to what to do with the ghost? After you make an attempt to identify who is doing the haunting, and you've determined that there is a haunting in your home, it's time to move forward.

If Your House IS Haunted...

The following are basic steps to take:

† Rule out the natural before you look at the supernatural: cold drafts, sudden breezes, or air pockets that shut doors can often be explained by poor ventilation, old windows, forced-air heating or cooling systems, or even poor insulation. Identify natural causes for strange noises. One woman I worked with many years ago swore she heard a far-away ghostly sound of a heart monitor and believed it was the spirit of a deceased relative who spent his final moments hooked up to all kinds of tubes and wires in a hospital. Two sleepless nights later, she discovered her smoke detector in a closed-off storage room in the basement had a dying battery, which emitted a low, steady heart-monitor sound.

The tapping noises you may hear could be anything from a faulty furnace to water pipes to acorns from a backyard tree hitting the roof on a windy day. Make a note of when and where the knocking or tapping occurs. Is it raining? Is it windy? Do you live in an apartment or condo that is above or below someone whose hobby may cause tapping noises—a woodworker, artist, or someone who is remodeling?

Those with keen olfactory senses may smell medicine, which may indicate a spirit who was ill before crossing over. Others may smell alcohol indicating a ghost who loved to kick a few back in his time. But be realistic and, again, look at natural causes before assuming the supernatural.

† When you are fairly certain that you have a ghost who is not welcome, it's time to take action. First, fear is a big motivator in doing nothing, and people fear what they do not understand. I must tell you, however, that you need to let go of all the crazy images you have in your mind left by scary movies. It is possible, but rare, to find any type of spirits that will cause you severe harm. Most are just lost, confused, mischievous, bitter, or looking for closure. I do believe in poltergeists and I do believe there are dark entities out there, but if it's that bad, you need a demonologist, not Mimi.

Once you let go of the fear, you can begin to take control. Got yourself together? Good. Now assert yourself. It seems silly the first time you try it, but introduce yourself, if you haven't already. Then tell them you are aware that they are here (sometimes, that is all they desire is acknowledgement). Then you must tell the spirit to leave, especially if that ghostie is causing mischief. Tell them every several days, if necessary. If they refuse, tell them the physical world belongs to the living. If you don't necessarily desire to cast them out altogether, stand firm and tell them, "This is my space, and your actions will not be tolerated. If you want to stay, you need to abide by the rules of the house." Then state your rules. Remember, many ghosts retain the same personality of their last incarnation. So once you get a feel for what type of person they were, you can anticipate their actions through their mannerisms, and know what works and what doesn't.

† Take a lighted white candle and walk the perimeters of each room. Visualize a white light of protection and state that only those who are invited are welcome. You can also state that ancestors and deceased relatives are welcome to stay, if that is your desire.

† Smudging, through the use of dried sage (some use cedar), is a more intense form of getting rid of spirits, or at least keeping them at bay. Smudging is a form of cleaning the "spiritual energy" in the house by lighting a bundle of the herb and allowing the smoke to permeate the home.

Sage bundles can be purchased from suppliers who carry spiritual goods. You can easily purchase sage or grow your own. Once it has been cut and dried, wrap it tightly with cotton string—I use embroidery floss—leaving the tip unbound. Light the sage bundle (some refer to it as a smudge stick) keeping an ashtray or small bowl of water with you. Some use an abalone shell. Go room to room and let the sage smoke permeate the home. Open the front door and the back door. Start in the front of the home, and move clockwise. With a left-to-right motion, wave the lit sage slowly and deliberately up, then down, once each time around doorways, windows, corners, archways, fireplaces, or other openings. Pay particular attention to vents, skylights, and other "passageways." Repeat the process on all floors, including the attic and the basement. If desired, say a short prayer or affirmation, such as "By the power of all that is sacred, I protect this dwelling and all its inhabitants from negative spirits."

† Salt has been known to be an excellent source for use in cleansing and to help in keeping ghosts away. The parts of a home where you feel energies are the most resistant or the most frightening should be dealt with first. Some believe that negative energies cannot exist in the same place as salt, based on ancient theories and practices. For centuries, salt has been used in ceremonies to cleanse everything from dwellings, to food (Orthodox Jews use it to keep meat kosher), to the body itself—Epsom salts are used in cleansing and in healing the body. Some prefer using sea salt versus iodized salt, but any salt will do. The salt can be put into

a bowl, uncovered, and placed under furniture, in closets, under the bed, or anywhere else you feel the strong sense of a not-so-nice presence.

Another away of using salt is to sprinkle it around the outside of the home or building, going clockwise until a full circle has been completed. Let me add that if you desire, repeating a prayer or saying, such as the one mentioned in the previous description of smudging, may give you an increasing feeling of power and protection. If you do decide to simply sprinkle the salt on the floor, remember that prolonged use may cause corrosion, so be careful. No more than three to five days should pass before you sweep up the salt—unless it's outdoors.

† Once you have interacted with a ghost, you become more adept at how to interpret his or her behavior. Also, the more experiences you have, the less fear you have in encountering ghosts. And now that you have a general idea on how to cleanse your home from the ghosts that you don't want hanging around—although I must emphasize that even cleansing may not get rid of them altogether, it will at least keep them quiet or dormant for awhile, it is time to look at what to do if you want to continue to learn about ghosts and gain some experience on a more advanced level.

Interested in Paranormal Investigations?

Hopefully, you are an avid reader of ghost books or are educating yourself on the paranormal through the Internet or by some other means, such as radio and television. Keep in mind that the ghost hunters on television also have a goal of keeping their ratings up, to avoid their shows being cancelled. They also have the luxury of having a professional film crew to accompany them wherever they go. Of course, this is not a typical setting for a real ghost hunt.

You will spend a lot of time, it seems, searching for that elusive ghost, in cold, damp basements, hot, musty attics, or outdoors in lousy weather. Some group directors or organizers will postpone an investigation in extremely bad weather—as they should—not only for safety reasons, but the fact that rain, heavy fog, or snow showers, even light snowflakes, may show up on film leading you to believe you've captured fascinating streaks, orbs, or ectoplasm. On the other hand, if the hunt is scheduled, and you have committed to attend, you need to be there. No-shows and latecomers are cause for removal of a group. Be realistic, do your homework, and don't wander off on your own.

Commonly Used Equipment

Voice recorder—Used for capturing EVPs, it's also handy to have when you're not a good note-taker. Homeowners or business owners who are experiencing the haunting may first give you a tour of the area or tell you about its history, if known. If you rely on your memory from an investigation you did a week prior, you will miss out on details. I invested in a good pair of stereo headphones, to listen to my recordings when I return. Listen at least twice—you may surprise yourself and catch a voice you didn't hear earlier.

Camera—There have been arguments for and against the use of digital cameras versus standard film cameras. Having both is also a good idea, say some investigators, as a variety of cameras can also support or help debunk anomalies captured, if two people get the same shot using two types of cameras.

EMF Detector—Electromagnetic Field Detectors reportedly pick up the energy fields of ghosts. At the beginning of an investigation, an EMF detector is sometimes used to take baseline readings of the area to pinpoint existing electromagnetic fields caused by power lines or appliances, to delineate between the energy of a physical item and that caused by ghosts. After establishing where the existing fields are, the EMF detector is then carried from room to room, to pick up the energy fields or "hot spots" where spirit activity may exist. I do believe that EMF detectors can be map, but are not the final answer.

Motion Sensors—Some investigators set up motion sensors in a specific room or rooms of a house, along with a camera placed on a tripod. The room can then be off-limits to investigators, to avoid tripping the sensor. A motion sensor can also be set up in an unoccupied dwelling, and then viewed from a remote area.

Thermal Scanner—Most thermal scanners are compact, hand-held devices that read temperature. Thermal scanners are used to instantly detect any remarkable changes (usually a drop of more than ten degrees of the ambient temperature) in a given area, possibly indicating a ghostly presence.

On the Hunt

Never go alone. If you are serious about ghost hunting, then learn all you can before heading out. Start by doing a complete walk-through of the area (unless it's a large area, like a cemetery). Get a feel for the general atmosphere first. You'll accomplish two things: First, you will allow the ghost(s) to pick up your energy and get introduced to you. Second, you can get a feel for which particular areas you seem drawn to, then hone in on those areas.

Bring a notebook and pen with you. Jot down the weather conditions, the time, the exact location, and anything odd that you feel and in what part of the house, cemetery, etc. Remember to record the events. You will become so involved in what you're doing you will not be able to rely on your memory to recapture those experiences.

Avoid aggression. When you are seeking ghosts, you are opening yourself up to a dimension that you may not be familiar with. Do not yell out, "Show yourself!" or "Bring it on!" There are dark entities out there that will be more than happy to answer the call.

Be realistic. It's great to be positive and have a good attitude, but do not have high expectations that you'll capture ghost pictures, EVPs, and everything else in one visit. Don't become frustrated if you get nothing. Even the most experienced investigators sometimes don't get a thing. When you least expect it, you will get something sooner or later.

Know your equipment. Ouija boards are tools. So are chainsaws. Both have a purpose and are guaranteed serious consequences when they get into the wrong hands.

Protect yourself. Wear sturdy shoes and a symbol of protection. It's OK to pray or ask for protection before, during, and after an investigation. If you don't want to include anything religious on the investigation, that's OK, too. But at least allow others to, if they desire.

Respect the dead. Always speak clearly and in a non-confrontational manner when addressing a ghost. If they are interacting with you, then they have a consciousness.

And they know what you are doing at their burial ground or place of death. "Please" and "thank you" may just be rewarded with an EVP or a cool photo in which you've captured something.

Bring back-up equipment. Carry a flashlight, and bring extra batteries and film. I always carry an additional camera (disposable), in case my good camera suddenly jams, or the battery dies out. Even experienced ghost hunters have all dealt with equipment failure at one time or another. Many seasoned ghost hunters have experienced inserting new batteries right there on site, only to have the energy drained out of them in a matter of a short time span. Could it be actual equipment failure, or could the perpetrator be the ghost?

Don't invest money on fancy gear. Motion detectors, thermal scanners, night vision goggles, and EMF readers are impressive, but are not absolutely necessary. You may want to start off with just the basics. You would be amazed at what you can capture on a basic recorder or with a simple camera.

Additional helpful hints

† When you ask the spirit questions, leave time in between to let them answer. Think about your questions beforehand. Ask them to describe what they're wearing—you may be able to determine from what time period they are. I sometimes ask them if they can see me, and if so, what color shirt I am wearing.

† Sometimes, you will be touched on the arm, back, or shoulder. If this happens, do not freak out and scream hysterically. You will get used to it, after you've done this a number of times. If it bothers you, simply tell the spirit,

aloud, "You are more than welcome to communicate with me, but please do not touch me."

† If you do decide to traipse through the cemetery and you see people visiting the grave of a loved one, save the investigation for another day, or venture out to another part of the cemetery. Respect the living and the dead, and remember you are on sacred ground.

† Now, if you are serious about paranormal investigating, ask yourself a few questions about what type of organization you may be interested in, and what talents or ideas you can offer to the group. Consider what type of member you want to be. Would you rather be part of a large, organized group that attends monthly meetings, regularly posts in messages boards, and maintains an updated web site? Usually larger groups have advanced equipment and can get booked into more "famous" haunts, such as those in restaurants, hotels, or similar. Maybe you prefer a smaller, closely knit group that seems to have good group dynamics.

Some folks consider a group of three or four the perfect size. Are you more interested in the technical side of ghost hunting, or do you tend to consider yourself sensitive? If you're not quite sure, that's okay, too. Once you've gained experience, you'll discover traits about yourself and gain confidence.

Some groups have no use for sensitives and mediums, relying strictly on equipment and tools. Others may select a person or two who they feel has a strong psychic or intuitive nature, to be the sensitive of the group. I believe a combination of the two makes a good system of checks and balances. I would have to agree with Lloyd Auerbach's opinion on the issue involving mediums on a ghost hunt. Auerbach, a popular parapsychologist, lecturer, and author, is considered by some to be a leading authority in paranormal research and investigations. He believes that paranormal investigators must branch out to include more than just equipment to investigate a haunting. Auerbach states, "The equipment is secondary and helps to correlate witness testimony with technology. The answers will be found in the middle somewhere...if you have no witnesses, and no psychics, you've got nothing."

I admit that when it comes to technical equipment, I am a minimalist. I have been on investigations involving a dozen or more participants with enough equipment to broadcast the half-time show at the Superbowl, and have come away with little more than a groan, a squeak, and an orb.

During a full-fledged investigation, it is imperative that you ask the client specific questions regarding the history of the property, the frequency of paranormal activity, and to get eyewitness accounts. I must admit that when I do a "loose" investigation (which I refer to as a ghost hunt, not an investigation) I dissuade myself from getting all of the history and background up front, and prefer to open up and see what my senses pick up first. This is called a cold investigation. After writing down my findings in my notebook, or recording them on a recorder, I let everything settle for a day or two. Then I delve into the history and background, and dig up a few witnesses to corroborate the story. Perhaps it is just the storyteller in me, or the fact that I love learning about the character of people and places, whether of this dimension or the next. Basically, keep an open mind regarding ghost stories, but don't believe everything you read on the Internet—always double check a secondary source, such as information found in libraries, police reports, or newspaper articles.

Well, that wraps it up. It has been a pleasure to present to you my strange encounters and to share the stories others have told to me. I extend to you my gratitude for allowing me to share my experiences and insight with you. Be safe and be well...and when it all gets too scary, leave the lights on. Happy hauntings to you and yours.

Glossary

Agent. A person (usually adolescent) who is the focus–and sometimes the cause–of poltergeist activity.

Anomalous Phenomena. Occurrences in an otherwise neutral environment that cannot be scientifically explained.

Apparition. A ghost or spirit in a visual form, as opposed to audible form, though the apparition may be accompanied by scent, voice, or sound.

Apport. An object that materializes from seemingly nowhere—usually associated with poltergeist activity. Common items associated with apportion include keys, coins, jewelry, and flowers.

Asport. An object from a known location that disappears and is found in a remote location without a valid explanation. See Teleportation.

Astral Projection. Similar to an out-of-body experience, where the person's astral form separates from his or her physical form. Often experienced in a dream state or by those who meditate and usually occurs when the person is completely aware, awake, and conscious.

Aura. A halo of energy seen as an illuminating ray of light (often seen in a variety of colors) surrounding living persons or animals.

Channeling. The process of a medium or clairvoyant receiving messages from a spirit using the spirit's voice and personality traits.

Clairaudience. "Clear hearing," or the ability to hear messages, voices, or sounds from spirits.

Clairsentience. "Clear sensing," or the ability to sense information from or about a spirit.

Clairvoyance. "Clear seeing," or the ability to see—psychically—spirits, information, written words, places, etc., relative to a given situation. Although in modern times, more of an all-encompassing word to mean psychic ability in general.

Clairvoyant. The person, usually a medium or sensitive, who displays clairvoyance.

Crisis apparition. An apparition of a living person who appears to family members, or others, hours or moments prior to death, accident, or severe illness.

Demon. An entity, often seen as a black mass, that wishes to inflict harm, negativity, or send out harmful thoughts. Not all demons are possessive, and may lie dormant for centuries, and not all evil spirits are demons.

Dematerialization. The vanishing, fading, or complete disappearance of a physical object.

Direct voice. A spirit voice that is heard directly from the spirit—as opposed to through the voice of a channeler, medium, or through a hypnotic state.

Ectoplasm. A fluid or semi-fluid substance, sometimes misty in appearance, often signaling the pre-appearance, existence, or post-appearance of an apparition. Ectoplasm is most often seen as green, but has also been reported as being darkish red or black.

Electronic Voice Phenomena (EVP). The sounds, voices, or noises captured on a recording device that comes from, or is associated with, a ghostly presence.

Elemental Spirits. Non-human nature spirits represented through trees, rivers and oceans, flora, fauna, the earth, etc. Most appear in the form of woodland creatures, nymphs, fae, or may possess unique animal traits. Associated with the four basic elements: earth, air, fire, and water.

Empath. A sensitive who feels or picks up on the feelings, personality, emotions, of the living or non-living.

Guide. A spirit who assists a person in various aspects of his or her life journey. Often interchanged with "guardian angel," though the two differ in that the guide or guides may assist in specific talents, abilities, skills, and traits, whereas guardian angels are associated with protection and intervention.

Haunting. Unreasonable or unexplained phenomena in the form of apparitions, scents, voices, levitation, lights, movements, or other signs indicative of supernatural occurrences, usually over an extended period of time.

Levitation. Raising or lifting a person or object without the use of physical means.

Materialization. The manifestation or appearance of a physical object without a reasonable or obvious explanation. Similar to apport, though the materialization is the process and the apport is the actual object.

Medium. A person who acts as the liaison between the living and the non-living. Sometimes used interchangeably with clairvoyant, channeler, psychic, or sensitive.

OBE or OOBE. Out of body experience. Similar to astral travel, though the person is fully conscious, awake, and experiences the sensation of being outside of their physical body.

Parapsychology. Referring to the scientific study and experimental and quantitative studies of paranormal phenomena. Formerly referred to as psychical research.

Past-life memories. Images or bits and pieces of information received by a person that may indicate occurrences in his or her previous life.

Phantasm. Visual appearance of an apparition, specter, ghost, or any type of mass that takes the shape or form of a person or animal.

PK. Shortened version of the word, psychokinesis. The ability to use the mind to influence or master physical change.

Poltergeist. German word meaning, "noisy ghost." Often, poltergeist activity centers around (or is caused by) those whose home is occupied by an adolescent. Poltergeists are often erroneously assumed to have a negative connotation.

Psychometry. The ability to pick up psychic information about a person by touching or holding a physical object belonging to that person.

Qualitative method. Approaching an investigation with the use of non-statistical methods, such as observations considered subjective or non-measurable, scientifically.

Quantitative method. Approaching an investigation using statistical data that can be measured scientifically.

Raps/Rappings. Knocking sounds emanating from walls, tables, or other means, usually signifying a spiritual presence. Coined in 1848, when the Fox sisters in Hydesville, New York gained worldwide attention by their communication with an entity whose body was buried in the basement of their home.

Remote viewing. The ability to see experiences taking place in a remote location.

Sensitive. A term used to describe a person who has the ability to sense specific areas of paranormal activity, the presence of a spirit, or other paranormal phenomena. Often used interchangeably with medium, psychic, or clairvoyant.

Shape-shifting. The transformation or manifestation into the form of an animal, person, or other entity other than one's self.

Sleep paralysis. A term used to describe the conscious state of being awake, yet unable to control the physical movement of one's body. Often associated with a feeling of being controlled or spellbound by an unseen entity.

Spiritualism. A belief system that advocates the communication of the living and the non-living. Spiritualism emerged in the late 1800s and increased in popularity following the Civil War and World War I, where widows and family members looked for ways of communicating with deceased relatives who died in battle.

Table-tipping. Also known as table turning, occurs in circle or séance, where the table may levitate, turn, or vibrate, indicating a spiritual presence.

Target. The person, place, or object that becomes the recipient to which the paranormal activity is aimed or directed.

Telekinesis. Using the mind, whether conscious or subconscious, to control, move, or manipulate physical objects.

Teleportation. The means of dematerialization of matter at one location, which materializes at another, usually instantaneously. Teleportation can be conscious or subconscious, and can occur through solid forms, such as walls, floors, stairs, or other physical barriers.

White noise. A sound formed by a combination of all frequencies. Similar to how white light is used to describe all different colors combined, white noise combines the frequencies of all sound. Often associated with paranormal occurrences in that it is believed that spirits can sometimes communicate through electrical currents, radio waves, computers, appliances, telephones, and televisions.

Bibliography

Andrews, Ted. *Animal-Speak*. St. Paul, Minnesota: Llewellyn Publications, 1998.

Aschenbrenner, Evelyn. "Tales from the Crypts: Digging up the dirt on Detroit's past." *Detroit Free Press*. November 3, 2005.

Author unknown. "Big Fountain for Detroit." *New York Times*. July 14, 1914.

Detroit Institute of Arts (www.dia.org). *American Art before 1950*. "The Court of Death." Rembrandt Peale, artist 1778-1860; Gift of George H. Scripps.

Doyle, Sir Arthur Conan. *The History of Spiritualism Vol. II*. United States: Book Tree, reprinted July 2007.

Farncombe, Judy. "The Sadness of Suicide, and Those Left Behind." *Psychic Tymes*. June 2007; Vol. 7, Issue No. 18.

Ferry, W. Hawkins. *The Buildings of Detroit: A History*. Detroit, Michigan: Wayne State University Press, 1968.

Hagman, Arthur, et al. 1970. *Oakland County Book of History, Sesquicentennial Edition [1820-1970]*. No publisher listed.

Hallowell, Bay. "Nail Figure." The Free Library of Detroit, www.thefreelibrary.com. (accessed December 27, 2007)

Kuclo, Marion (a/k/a Gundella). *Michigan Haunts and Hauntings, 3rd Edition*. Lansing, Michigan: Thunder Bay Press, 1997. (Updated, in memoriam, dedicated to the memory of the Green Witch Gundella, 1930-1993).

McCraw, Jim. "Ghosts of Detroit's Past in Ford's Old Buildings." *New York Times*. October 15, 1999.

McMullin, Stanley Edward. *Anatomy of a Séance: A History of Spirit Communication in Central Canada*. Kingston, Ontario: McGill-Queen's University Press, 2004.

Nolan, Jenny. "Prohibition: How Detroit Became a Bootlegger's Dream Town." *Rearview Mirror*. Detroit, Michigan: *The Detroit News*, June 15, 1999.

Owl, Lillian. *Ghosts 101: Haunting First Aid*. eBook, bookbooters.com

Visitor Guide 2008. "The Henry Ford." Dearborn, Michigan. September 2007, no publisher listed.

Wren's Cottage, Greenfield Village Memories, wrenscottage. com, 2008.